Eat That Frog!

Other Books by Brian Tracy

Eat That Frog!

21 Great Ways to Stop Procrastinating and Get More Done in Less Time

Brian Tracy

BERRETT-KOEHLER PUBLISHERS, INC.
San Francisco
a BK Life book

Berrett-Koehler Publishers, Inc.
235 Montgomery Street, Suite 650
San Francisco, CA 94104-2916
Tel: (415) 288-0260   Fax: (415) 362-2512   www.bkconnection.com

Ordering Information
Quantity sales. Special discounts are available on quantity purchases by corporations, associations, and others. For details, contact the "Special Sales Department" at the Berrett-Koehler address above.
Individual sales. Berrett-Koehler publications are available through most bookstores. They can also be ordered directly from Berrett-Koehler: Tel: (800) 929-2929; Fax: (802) 864-7626; http://www.bkconnection.com.
Orders for college textbook/course adoption use. Please contact Berrett-Koehler: Tel: (800) 929-2929; Fax: (802) 864-7626.
Orders by U.S. trade bookstores and wholesalers. Please contact Ingram Publisher Services, Tel: (800) 509-4887; Fax: (800) 838-1149; E-mail: customer.service@ingram publisherservices.com; or visit www.ingrampublisherservices.com/Ordering for details about electronic ordering.

Berrett-Koehler and the BK logo are registered trademarks of Berrett-Koehler Publishers, Inc.

Printed in the United States of America

Berrett-Koehler books are printed on long-lasting acid-free paper. When it is available, we choose paper that has been manufactured by environmentally responsible processes. These may include using trees grown in sustainable forests, incorporating recycled paper, minimizing chlorine in bleaching, or recycling the energy produced at the paper mill.

Library of Congress Cataloging-in-Publication Data
Tracy, Brian.
  Eat that frog! : 21 great ways to stop procrastinating and get more done in less time / by Brian Tracy. — 2nd ed.
    p. cm.
  ISBN: 978-1-57675-422-1 (pbk.)
  1. Procrastination. I. Title.
  BF637.P76T73 2006
  640'.43—dc22   2006021172

Copyediting and proofreading by PeopleSpeak.
Book design and composition by Beverly Butterfield, Girl of the West Productions.
Indexing by Rachel Rice.
Cover design by Leslie Waltzer, Crowfoot Design.

SECOND EDITION
11 10 09 08   10 9 8 7 6 5 4 3

To my remarkable daughter Catherine,

an amazing girl with a wonderful mind

and an incredible future lying before her

Contents

Preface

Thank you for picking up this book. I hope these ideas help you as much as they have helped me and thousands of others. In fact, I hope that this book changes your life forever.

There is never enough time to do everything you have to do. You are literally swamped with work and personal responsibilities, projects, stacks of magazines to read, and piles of books you intend to get to one of these days—as soon as you get caught up.

But the fact is that you are *never* going to get caught up. You will never get on top of your tasks. You will never get far enough ahead to be able to get to all those books, magazines, and leisure time activities that you dream of.

And forget about solving your time management problems by becoming more productive. No matter how many personal productivity techniques you master, there will always be more to do than you can ever accomplish in the time you have available to you, no matter how much it is.

You can get control of your time and your life only by changing the way you think, work, and deal with the never-ending river of responsibilities that flows over you each day. You can get control of your tasks and activities only to the degree that you stop doing some things and start spending more time on the few activities that can really make a difference in your life.

I have studied time management for more than thirty years. I have immersed myself in the works of Peter Drucker, Alec Mackenzie, Alan Lakein, Stephen Covey, and many, many others. I have read hundreds of books and thousands of articles on personal efficiency and effectiveness. This book is the result.

Each time I came across a good idea, I tried it out in my own work and personal life. If it worked, I incorporated it into my talks and seminars and taught it to others.

Galileo once wrote, "You cannot teach a man anything; you can only help him find it within himself."

Depending upon your level of knowledge and experience, these ideas may sound familiar. This book will bring them to a higher level of awareness. When you learn and apply these methods and techniques over and over until they become habits, you will alter the course of your life in a very positive way.

The Power of Written Goals

Let me tell you something about myself and the origins of this little book. I started off in life with few advantages, aside from a curious mind. I did poorly in school and left without graduating. I worked at laboring jobs for several years. My future did not appear promising.

As a young man, I got a job on a tramp freighter and went off to see the world. For eight years, I traveled and worked and then traveled some more, eventually visiting more than eighty countries on five continents.

When I could no longer find a laboring job, I got into sales, knocking on doors, working on straight commission. I struggled from sale to sale until I began looking around me and asking, "Why is it that other people are doing better than I am?"

Then I did something that changed my life. I began to ask successful people what they were doing that enabled them to be more productive and earn more money than me. And they told me. I did what they advised me to do, and my sales went up. Eventually, I became so successful that I was made a sales manager. As a sales manager, I used the same strategy. I asked successful managers what they did to achieve such great results, and when they told me, I did it myself. In no time at all, I began to get the same results they did.

This process of learning and applying what I had learned changed my life. I am still amazed at how simple and obvious it is. Just find out what other successful people do and do the same things until you get the same results. Learn from the experts. Wow! What an idea.

Success Is Predictable

Simply put, some people are doing better than others because they do things differently and they do the right things right. Especially, successful, happy, prosperous people use their time far, far better than the average person.

Coming from an unsuccessful background, I had developed deep feelings of inferiority and inadequacy. I had fallen into the mental trap of assuming that people who were doing better than me were actually better than me. What I learned was that this was not necessarily true. They were just doing things *differently,* and what they had learned to do, within reason, I could learn as well.

This was a revelation to me. I was both amazed and excited with this discovery. I still am. I realized that I could change my life and achieve almost any goal I could set if I just found out what others were doing in that area and then did it myself until I got the same results they were getting.

Within one year of starting in sales, I was a top salesman. A year later I was made a manager. Within three years, I became a vice president in charge of a ninety-five-person sales force in six countries. I was twenty-five years old.

Over the years, I have worked in twenty-two different jobs; started and built several companies; earned a business degree from a major university; learned to speak French, German, and Spanish; and been a speaker, trainer, or consultant for more than 1,000 companies. I currently give talks and seminars to more than 250,000 people each year, with audiences as large as 20,000 people.

A Simple Truth

Throughout my career, I have discovered and rediscovered a simple truth. The ability to concentrate single-mindedly on your most important task, to do it well and to finish it completely, is the key to great success, achievement, respect, status, and happiness in life. This key insight is the heart and soul of this book.

This book is written to show you how to get ahead more rapidly in your career and to simultaneously enrich your personal life. These pages contain the twenty-one most powerful principles on personal effectiveness I have ever discovered.

These methods, techniques, and strategies are practical, proven, and fast acting. In the interest of time, I do not dwell on the various psychological or emotional explanations for procrastination or poor time management. There are no lengthy departures into theory or research. What you will learn are specific actions you can take immediately to get better, faster results in your work and to increase your happiness.

Every idea in this book is focused on increasing your overall levels of productivity, performance, and output and on making you more valuable in whatever you do. You can apply many of these ideas to your personal life as well.

Each of these twenty-one methods and techniques is complete in itself. All are necessary. One strategy might be effective in one situation and another might apply to another task. All together, these twenty-one ideas represent a smorgasbord of personal effectiveness techniques that you can use at any time, in any order or sequence that makes sense to you at the moment.

The key to success is action. These principles work to bring about fast, predictable improvements in performance and results. The faster you learn and apply them, the faster you will move ahead in your career— guaranteed!

There will be no limit to what you can accomplish when you learn how to *Eat That Frog!*

Brian Tracy
Solana Beach, California
October 2006

Introduction: Eat That Frog

This is a wonderful time to be alive. There have never been more possibilities and opportunities for you to achieve more of your goals than exist today. As perhaps never before in human history, you are actually drowning in options. In fact, there are so many good things that you can do that your ability to decide among them may be the critical determinant of what you accomplish in life.

If you are like most people today, you are overwhelmed with too much to do and too little time. As you struggle to get caught up, new tasks and responsibilities just keep rolling in, like the waves of the ocean. Because of this, you will never be able to do everything you have to do. You will never be caught up. You will always be behind in some of your tasks and responsibilities, and probably in many of them.

The Need to Be Selective

For this reason, and perhaps more than ever before, your ability to select your most important task at each moment, and then to get started on that task and to get it done both quickly and well, will probably have more of an impact on your success than any other quality or skill you can develop.

An average person who develops the habit of setting clear priorities and getting important tasks completed

ircles around a genius who talks a lot
ful plans but who gets very little done.

The Truth about Frogs

Mark Twain once said that if the first thing you do each
morning is to eat a live frog, you can go through the day
with the satisfaction of knowing that that is probably the
worst thing that is going to happen to you all day long.

Your "frog" is your biggest, most important task, the
one you are most likely to procrastinate on if you don't
do something about it. It is also the one task that can
have the greatest positive impact on your life and results
at the moment.

The first rule of frog eating is this:
If you have to eat two frogs, eat the ugliest one first.

This is another way of saying that if you have two
important tasks before you, start with the biggest, hardest, and most important task first. Discipline yourself to
begin immediately and then to persist until the task is
complete before you go on to something else.

Think of this as a test. Treat it like a personal challenge. Resist the temptation to start with the easier
task. Continually remind yourself that one of the most
important decisions you make each day is what you
will do immediately and what you will do later, if you
do it at all.

The second rule of frog eating is this:
If you have to eat a live frog at all, it doesn't pay
to sit and look at it for very long.

The key to reaching high levels of performance and productivity is to develop the lifelong habit of tackling your major task first thing each morning. You must develop the routine of "eating your frog" before you do anything else and without taking too much time to think about it.

Take Action Immediately

In study after study of men and women who get paid more and promoted faster, the quality of "action orientation" stands out as the most observable and consistent behavior they demonstrate in everything they do. Successful, effective people are those who launch directly into their major tasks and then discipline themselves to work steadily and single-mindedly until those tasks are complete.

In our world, and especially in our business world, you are paid and promoted for getting specific, measurable results. You are paid for making a valuable contribution and especially for making the most important contribution that is expected of you.

"Failure to execute" is one of the biggest problems in organizations today. Many people confuse activity with accomplishment. They talk continually, hold endless meetings, and make wonderful plans, but in the final analysis, no one does the job and gets the results required.

Develop the Habits of Success

Your success in life and work will be determined by the kinds of habits that you develop over time. The habit of setting priorities, overcoming procrastination, and getting on with your most important task is a mental and physical skill. As such, this habit is learnable through practice and repetition, over and over again, until it locks into your subconscious mind and becomes a permanent part of your behavior. Once it becomes a habit, it becomes both automatic and easy to do.

This habit of starting and completing important tasks has an immediate and continuous payoff. You are designed mentally and emotionally in such a way that task completion gives you a positive feeling. It makes you happy. It makes you feel like a winner.

Whenever you complete a task of any size or importance, you feel a surge of energy, enthusiasm, and self-esteem. The more important the completed task, the happier, more confident, and more powerful you feel about yourself and your world.

The completion of an important task triggers the release of *endorphins* in your brain. These endorphins give you a natural "high." The endorphin rush that follows successful completion of any task makes you feel more positive, personable, creative, and confident.

Develop a Positive Addiction

Here is one of the most important of the so-called secrets of success. You can actually develop a "positive addiction" to endorphins and to the feeling of enhanced clarity, confidence, and competence that they trigger. When you develop this addiction, you will, at an unconscious level, begin to organize your life in such a way that you are continually starting and completing ever more important tasks and projects. You will actually become addicted, in a very positive sense, to success and contribution.

One of the keys to your living a wonderful life, having a successful career, and feeling terrific about yourself is to develop the habit of starting and finishing important jobs. When you do, this behavior will take on a power of its own and you'll find it easier to complete important tasks than not to complete them.

No Shortcuts

You remember the story of the man who stops a musician on a street in New York and asks how he can get to Carnegie Hall. The musician replies, "Practice, man, practice."

Practice is the key to mastering any skill. Fortunately, your mind is like a muscle. It grows stronger and more capable with use. With practice, you can learn any behavior or develop any habit that you consider either desirable or necessary.

The Three Ds of New Habit Formation

You need three key qualities to develop the habits of focus and concentration, which are all learnable. They are decision, discipline, and determination.

First, make a *decision* to develop the habit of task completion. Second, *discipline* yourself to practice the principles you are about to learn over and over until they become automatic. And third, back everything you do with *determination* until the habit is locked in and becomes a permanent part of your personality.

Visualize Yourself as You Want to Be

There is a special way that you can accelerate your progress toward becoming the highly productive, effective, efficient person that you want to be. It consists of your thinking continually about the rewards and benefits of being an action-oriented, fast-moving, and focused person. See yourself as the kind of person who gets important jobs done quickly and well on a consistent basis.

Your mental picture of yourself has a powerful effect on your behavior. Visualize yourself as the person you intend to be in the future. Your self-image, the way you see yourself on the inside, largely determines your performance on the outside. All improvements in your *outer* life begin with improvements on the *inside,* in your mental pictures.

You have a virtually unlimited ability to learn and develop new skills, habits, and abilities. When you train yourself, through repetition and practice, to overcome procrastination and get your most important tasks completed quickly, you will move yourself onto the fast track in your life and career and step on the accelerator.

Eat That Frog!

1
Set the Table

There is one quality that one must possess to win, and that is definiteness of purpose, the knowledge of what one wants and a burning desire to achieve it.

NAPOLEON HILL

Before you can determine your "frog" and get on with the job of eating it, you have to decide exactly what you want to achieve in each area of your life. *Clarity* is perhaps the most important concept in personal productivity. The number one reason why some people get more work done faster is because they are absolutely clear about their goals and objectives, and they don't deviate from them. The greater clarity you have regarding what you want and the steps you will have to take to achieve it, the easier it will be for you to overcome procrastination, eat your frog, and complete the task before you.

A major reason for procrastination and lack of motivation is vagueness, confusion, and fuzzy-mindedness about what you are trying to do and in what order and for what reason. You must avoid this common condition with all your strength by striving for ever greater clarity in your major goals and tasks.

Here is a great rule for success:
Think on paper.

Only about 3 percent of adults have clear, written goals. These people accomplish five and ten times as much as people of equal or better education and ability but who, for whatever reason, have never taken the time to write out exactly what they want.

There is a powerful formula for setting and achieving goals that you can use for the rest of your life. It consists of seven simple steps. Any one of these steps can double and triple your productivity if you are not currently using it. Many of my graduates have increased their incomes dramatically in a matter of a few years, or even a few months, with this simple, seven-part method.

Step one: *Decide exactly what you want.* Either decide for yourself or sit down with your boss and discuss your goals and objectives until you are crystal clear about what is expected of you and in what order of priority. It is amazing how many people are working away, day after day, on low-value tasks because they have not had this critical discussion with their managers.

One of the very worst uses of time is to do
something very well that need not be done at all.

Stephen Covey says, "Before you begin scrambling up the ladder of success, make sure that it is leaning against the right building."

Step two: *Write it down.* Think on paper. When you write down a goal, you crystallize it and give it tangible form. You create something that you can touch and see. On the other hand, a goal or objective that is not in writing is merely a wish or a fantasy. It has no energy behind it. Unwritten goals lead to confusion, vagueness, misdirection, and numerous mistakes.

Step three: *Set a deadline on your goal; set subdeadlines if necessary.* A goal or decision without a deadline has no urgency. It has no real beginning or end. Without a definite deadline accompanied by the assignment or acceptance of specific responsibilities for completion, you will naturally procrastinate and get very little done.

Step four: *Make a list of everything that you can think of that you are going to have to do to achieve your goal.* As you think of new activities, add them to your list. Keep building your list until it is complete. A list gives you a visual picture of the larger task or objective. It gives you a track to run on. It dramatically increases the likelihood that you will achieve your goal as you have defined it and on schedule.

Step five: *Organize the list into a plan.* Organize your list by priority and sequence. Take a few minutes to decide what you need to do first and what you can do later. Decide what has to be done before something else and what needs to be done afterward. Even better, lay out your plan visually in the form of a series of boxes and circles on a sheet of paper, with lines and arrows showing the relationship of each task to each other task.

You'll be amazed at how much easier it is to achieve your goal when you break it down into individual tasks.

With a written goal and an organized plan of action, you will be far more productive and efficient than people who are carrying their goals around in their minds.

Step six: *Take action on your plan immediately.* Do something. Do anything. An average plan vigorously executed is far better than a brilliant plan on which nothing is done. For you to achieve any kind of success, execution is everything.

Step seven: *Resolve to do something every single day that moves you toward your major goal.* Build this activity into your daily schedule. You may decide to read a specific number of pages on a key subject. You may call on a specific number of prospects or customers. You may engage in a specific period of physical exercise. You may learn a certain number of new words in a foreign language. Whatever it is, you must never miss a day.

Keep pushing forward. Once you start moving, keep moving. Don't stop. This decision, this discipline alone, can dramatically increase your speed of goal accomplishment and boost your personal productivity.

The Power of Written Goals

Clear written goals have a wonderful effect on your thinking. They motivate you and galvanize you into action. They stimulate your creativity, release your energy, and help you to overcome procrastination as much as any other factor.

Goals are the fuel in the furnace of achievement. The bigger your goals and the clearer they are, the more excited you become about achieving them. The more you think about your goals, the greater become your inner drive and desire to accomplish them.

Think about your goals and review them daily. Every morning when you begin, take action on the most important task you can accomplish to achieve your most important goal at the moment.

EAT THAT FROG!

1. Take a clean sheet of paper right now and make a list of ten goals you want to accomplish in the next year. Write your goals as though a year has already passed and they are now a reality.

Use the present tense, positive voice, and first person so that they are immediately accepted by your subconscious mind. For example, you could write. "I earn x number of dollars per year" or "I weigh x number of pounds" or "I drive such and such a car."

2. Review your list of ten goals and select the one goal that, if you achieved it, would have the greatest positive impact on your life. Whatever that goal is, write it on a separate sheet of paper, set a deadline, make a plan, take action on your plan, and then do something every single day that moves you toward that goal. This exercise alone could change your life!

2
Plan Every Day in Advance

Planning is bringing the future into the present
so that you can do something about it now.
ALAN LAKEIN

You have heard the old question, "How do you eat an elephant?" The answer is "One bite at a time!"

How do you eat your biggest, ugliest frog? The same way; you break it down into specific step-by-step activities and then you start on the first one.

Your mind, your ability to think, plan, and decide, is your most powerful tool for overcoming procrastination and increasing your productivity. Your ability to set goals, make plans, and take action on them determines the course of your life. The very act of thinking and planning unlocks your mental powers, triggers your creativity, and increases your mental and physical energies.

Conversely, as Alec Mackenzie wrote, *"Taking action without thinking things through is a prime source of problems."*

Your ability to make good plans before you act is a measure of your overall competence. The better the plan you have, the easier it is for you to overcome procrastination, to get started, to eat your frog, and then to keep going.

Increase Your Return on Energy

One of your top goals at work should be for you to get the highest possible return on your investment of mental, emotional, and physical energy. The good news is that every minute spent in planning saves as many as ten minutes in execution. It takes only about 10 to 12 minutes for you to plan out your day, but this small investment of time will save you up to two hours (100 to 120 minutes) in wasted time and diffused effort throughout the day.

You may have heard of the Six-P Formula. It says, "Proper Prior Planning Prevents Poor Performance."

When you consider how helpful planning can be in increasing your productivity and performance, it is amazing how few people practice it every single day. And planning is really quite simple to do. All you need is a piece of paper and a pen. The most sophisticated Palm Pilot, computer program, or time planner is based on the same principle. It is based on your sitting down and making a list of everything you have to do before you begin.

Two Extra Hours per Day

Always work from a list. When something new comes up, add it to the list before you do it. You can increase your productivity and output by 25 percent or more—about two hours a day—from the first day that you begin working consistently from a list.

Make your list the night before for the workday ahead. Move everything that you have not yet accomplished onto your list for the coming day, and then add everything that you have to do the next day. When you make your list the night before, your subconscious mind will work on your list all night long while you sleep. Often you will wake up with great ideas and insights that you can use to get your job done faster and better than you had initially thought.

The more time you take to make written lists of everything you have to do, in advance, the more effective and efficient you will be.

Different Lists for Different Purposes

You need different lists for different purposes. First, you should create a *master list* on which you write down everything you can think of that you want to do sometime in the future. This is the place where you capture every idea and every new task or responsibility that comes up. You can sort out the items later.

Second, you should have a *monthly list* that you make at the end of the month for the month ahead. This may contain items transferred from your master list.

Third, you should have a *weekly list* where you plan your entire week in advance. This is a list that is under construction as you go through the current week.

This discipline of systematic time planning can be very helpful to you. Many people have told me that the habit of taking a couple of hours at the end of each week to plan the coming week has increased their productivity dramatically and changed their lives completely. This technique will work for you as well.

Finally, you should transfer items from your monthly and weekly lists onto your *daily list*. These are the specific activities that you are going to accomplish the following day.

As you work through the day, tick off the items on your list as you complete them. This activity gives you a visual picture of accomplishment. It generates a feeling of success and forward motion. Seeing yourself working progressively through your list motivates and energizes you. It raises your self-esteem and self-respect. Steady, visible progress propels you forward and helps you to overcome procrastination.

Planning a Project

When you have a project of any kind, begin by making a list of every step that you will have to complete to finish the project from beginning to end. Organize the steps by priority and sequence. Lay out the project in front of you on paper or on a computer so that you can see every step and task. Then go to work on one task at a time. You will be amazed at how much you get done in this way.

As you work through your lists, you will feel more and more effective and powerful. You will feel more in control of your life. You will be naturally motivated to do even more. You will think better and more creatively, and you will get more and better insights that enable you to do your work even faster.

As you work steadily through your lists, you will develop a sense of positive forward momentum that enables you to overcome procrastination. This feeling of progress gives you more energy and keeps you going throughout the day.

One of the most important rules of personal effectiveness is the *10/90 Rule.* This rule says that the first 10 percent of time that you spend planning and organizing your work before you begin will save you as much as 90 percent of the time in getting the job done once you get started. You only have to try this rule once to prove it to yourself.

When you plan each day in advance, you will find it much easier to get going and to keep going. The work will go faster and smoother than ever before. You will feel more powerful and competent. You will get more done faster than you thought possible. Eventually, you will become *unstoppable.*

EAT THAT FROG!

1. Begin today to plan every day, week, and month in advance. Take a notepad or sheet of paper (or use your PDA or BlackBerry) and make a list of everything you have to do in the next twenty-four hours. Add to your list as new items come up. Make a list of all your projects, the big multitask jobs that are important to your future.

2. Lay out each of your major goals, projects, or tasks by *priority*, what is most important, and by *sequence*, what has to be done first, what comes second, and so forth. Start with the end in mind and work backward.

Think on paper! Always work from a list. You'll be amazed at how much more productive you become and how much easier it is to eat your frog.

3 Apply the 80/20 Rule to Everything

We always have time enough,
if we will but use it aright.

JOHANN WOLFGANG VON GOETHE

The 80/20 Rule is one of the most helpful of all concepts of time and life management. It is also called the "Pareto Principle" after its founder, the Italian economist Vilfredo Pareto, who first wrote about it in 1895. Pareto noticed that people in his society seemed to divide naturally into what he called the "vital few," the top 20 percent in terms of money and influence, and the "trivial many," the bottom 80 percent.

He later discovered that virtually all economic activity was subject to this principle as well. For example, this principle says that 20 percent of your activities will account for 80 percent of your results, 20 percent of your customers will account for 80 percent of your sales, 20 percent of your products or services will account for 80 percent of your profits, 20 percent of your tasks will account for 80 percent of the value of what you do, and so on. This means that if you have a list of ten items to do, two of those items will turn out to be worth five or ten times or more than the other eight items put together.

Number of Tasks versus Importance of Tasks

Here is an interesting discovery. Each of the ten tasks may take the same amount of time to accomplish. But one or two of those tasks will contribute five or ten times the value of any of the others.

Often, one item on a list of ten tasks that you have to do can be worth more than all the other *nine* items put together. This task is invariably the frog that you should eat first.

Can you guess on which items the average person is most likely to procrastinate? The sad fact is that most people procrastinate on the top 10 or 20 percent of items that are the most valuable and important, the "vital few." They busy themselves instead with the least important 80 percent, the "trivial many" that contribute very little to results.

Focus on Activities, Not Accomplishments

You often see people who appear to be busy all day long but seem to accomplish very little. This is almost always because they are busy working on tasks that are of low value while they are procrastinating on the one or two activities that, if they completed them quickly and well, could make a real difference to their companies and to their careers.

The most valuable tasks you can do each day are often the hardest and most complex. But the payoff and rewards for completing these tasks efficiently can be tremendous. For this reason, you must adamantly refuse to work on tasks in the bottom 80 percent while you still have tasks in the top 20 percent left to be done.

Before you begin work, always ask yourself, "Is this task in the top 20 percent of my activities or in the bottom 80 percent?"

Rule: Resist the temptation to clear up small things first.

Remember, whatever you choose to do over and over eventually becomes a habit that is hard to break. If you choose to start your day working on low-value tasks, you will soon develop the habit of always starting and working on low-value tasks. This is not the kind of habit you want to develop or keep.

The hardest part of any important task is getting started on it in the first place. Once you actually begin work on a valuable task, you will be naturally motivated to continue. A part of your mind loves to be busy working on significant tasks that can really make a difference. Your job is to feed this part of your mind continually.

Motivate Yourself

Just *thinking* about starting and finishing an important task motivates you and helps you to overcome procrastination. The fact is that the amount of time required to complete an important job is often the same as the time required to do an unimportant job. The difference is that you get a tremendous feeling of pride and satisfaction from the completion of something valuable and significant. However, when you complete a low-value task using the same amount of time and energy, you get little or no satisfaction at all.

Time management is really *life* management, personal management. It is really taking control of the *sequence of events*. Time management is having control over what you do next. And you are always free to choose the task that you will do next. Your ability to choose between the important and the unimportant is the key determinant of your success in life and work.

Effective, productive people discipline themselves to start on the most important task that is before them. They force themselves to eat that frog, whatever it is. As a result, they accomplish vastly more than the average person and are much happier as a result. This should be your way of working as well.

EAT THAT FROG!

1. Make a list of all the key goals, activities, projects, and responsibilities in your life today. Which of them are, or could be, in the top 10 or 20 percent of tasks that represent, or could represent, 80 or 90 percent of your results?

2. Resolve today that you are going to spend more and more of your time working in those few areas that can really make a difference in you life and career and less and less time on lower value activities.

4 Consider the Consequences

Every great man has become great,
every successful man has succeeded,
in proportion as he has confined his
powers to one particular channel.
ORISON SWETT MARDEN

The mark of the superior thinker is his or her ability to accurately predict the consequences of doing or not doing something. The potential consequences of any task or activity are the key determinants of how important a task really is to you and to your company. This way of evaluating the significance of a task is how you determine what your next frog really is.

Dr. Edward Banfield of Harvard University, after more than fifty years of research, concluded that "long-time perspective" is the most accurate single predictor of upward social and economic mobility in America.*Long-time perspective turns out to be more important than family background, education, race, intelligence, connections, or virtually any other single factor in determining your success in life and at work.

Your attitude toward time, your "time horizon," has an enormous impact on your behavior and your choices.

People who take a long view of their lives and careers always seem to make much better decisions about their time and activities than people who give very little thought to the future.

> Rule: Long-term thinking improves short-term decision making.

Successful people have a clear *future orientation*. They think five, ten, and twenty years out into the future. They analyze their choices and behaviors in the present to make sure that what they are doing today is consistent with the long-term future that they desire.

Make Better Decisions about Time

In your work, having a clear idea of what is really important to you in the long term makes it much easier for you to make better decisions about your priorities in the short term.

By definition, something that is important has long-term potential consequences. Something that is unimportant has few or no long-term potential consequences. Before starting on anything, you should always ask yourself, *"What are the potential consequences of doing or not doing this task?"*

> Rule: Future intent influences and often determines present actions.

The clearer you are about your future intentions, the greater influence that clarity will have on what you do in the moment. With a clear long-term vision, you are much more capable of evaluating an activity in the present to ensure that it is consistent with where you truly want to end up.

Think about the Long Term

Successful people are those who are willing to delay gratification and make sacrifices in the short term so that they can enjoy far greater rewards in the long term. Unsuccessful people, on the other hand, think more about short-term pleasure and immediate gratification while giving little thought to the long-term future.

Denis Waitley, a motivational speaker, says, "Losers try to escape from their fears and drudgery with activities that are tension-relieving. Winners are motivated by their desires toward activities that are goal-achieving." For example, coming into work earlier, reading regularly in your field, taking courses to improve your skills, and focusing on high-value tasks in your work will all combine to have an enormous positive impact on your future. On the other hand, coming into work at the last moment, reading the newspaper, drinking coffee, and socializing with your coworkers may seem fun and enjoyable in the short term but inevitably leads to lack of promotion, underachievement, and frustration in the long term.

If a task or activity has large potential positive consequences, make it a top priority and get started on it immediately. If something can have large potential negative consequences if it is not done quickly and well, that becomes a top priority as well. Whatever your frog is, resolve to gulp it down first thing.

Motivation requires *motive*. The greater the potential positive impact that an action or behavior of yours can have on your life, once you define it clearly, the more motivated you will be to overcome procrastination and get it done quickly.

Keep yourself focused and forward moving by continually starting and completing those tasks that can make a major difference to your company and to your future.

The time is going to pass anyway. The only question is how you use it and where you are going to end up at the end of the weeks and months that pass. And where you end up is largely a matter of the amount of consideration you give to the likely consequences of your actions in the short term.

Thinking continually about the potential consequences of your choices, decisions, and behaviors is one of the very best ways to determine your true priorities in your work and personal life.

Obey the Law of Forced Efficiency

The law of Forced Efficiency says that "There is never enough time to do everything, but there is always enough time to do the most important thing." Put another way, you cannot eat every tadpole and frog in the pond, but you can eat the biggest and ugliest one, and that will be enough, at least for the time being.

When you're running out of time and know that the consequences of not completing a key task or project can be really serious, you always seem to find the time to get it done, often at the very last minute. You start early, you stay late, and you drive yourself to complete the job rather than to face the unpleasantness that would follow if you didn't complete it within the time limit.

**Rule: There will never be enough time
to do everything you have to do.**

The average person in business today, especially a manager in the age of cutbacks, is working at 110 to 130 percent of capacity. And the jobs and responsibilities just keep piling up. We all have stacks of reading material we still have to go through. One recent study concluded that the average executive has 300 to 400 hours of reading and projects backlogged at home and at the office.

What this means is that you will never be caught up. Get that wishful idea out of your mind. All you can hope for is to be on top of your most important responsibilities. The others will just have to wait.

Deadlines Are an Excuse

Many people say that they work better under the pressure of deadlines. Unfortunately, years of research indicate that this is seldom true.

Under the pressure of deadlines, often self-created through procrastination, people suffer greater stress, make more mistakes, and have to redo more tasks than under any other conditions. Often the mistakes that people make when working under tight deadlines lead to defects and cost overruns that lead to substantial financial losses in the long term. Sometimes a job actually takes much longer to complete when people rush to get it done at the last minute and then have to redo it.

It is much better to plan your time carefully in advance and then build in a sizable buffer to compensate for unexpected delays and diversions. However much time you think a task will take, add on another 20 percent or more, or make a game of getting the job done well in advance of the deadline. You will be amazed at how much more relaxed you are and how much better a job you do.

Three Questions for Maximum Productivity

You can use three questions on a regular basis to keep yourself focused on completing your most important tasks on schedule. The first question is, *"What are my highest value activities?"* Put another way, what are the biggest frogs that you have to eat to make the greatest contribution to your organization? to your family? to your life in general?

This is one of the most important questions you can ask and answer. What are your highest-value activities? First, think this through for yourself. Then, ask your boss. Ask your coworkers and subordinates. Ask your friends and family. Like focusing the lens of a camera, you must be crystal clear about your highest-value activities before you begin work.

The second question you can ask continually is, *"What can I and only I do that if done well will make a real difference?"* This question came from the late Peter Drucker, the management guru. It is one of the best of all questions for achieving personal effectiveness. What can you and only you do that if done well can make a real difference?

This is something that only you can do. If you don't do it, it won't be done by someone else. But if you do do it and you do it well, it can really make a difference to your life and your career. What is this particular frog for you?

Every hour of every day, you can ask yourself this question and come up with a specific answer. Your job is to be clear about the answer and then to start and work on this task before anything else.

The third question you can ask is, *"What is the most valuable use of my time right now?"* In other words, "What is my biggest frog of all *at this moment?"*

This is the core question of time management. Answering this question correctly is the key to overcoming procrastination and becoming a highly productive person. Every hour of every day, one task represents the most valuable use of your time at that moment. Your job is to ask yourself this question, over and over again, and to always be working on the answer to it, whatever it is.

Do first things first and second things not at all. As Goethe said, *"Things that matter most must never be at the mercy of things that matter least."*

The more accurate your answers are to these three questions, the easier it will be for you to set clear priorities, to overcome procrastination, and to get started on that one activity that represents the most valuable use of your time.

EAT THAT FROG!

1. Review your list of tasks, activities, and projects regularly. Continually ask yourself, "Which one project or activity, if I did it in an excellent and timely fashion, would have the greatest positive consequences in my work or personal life?"

2. Determine the most important thing you could be doing every hour of every day, and then discipline yourself to work continually on the most valuable use of your time. What is this for you right now?

Whatever it is that can help you the most, set it as a goal, make a plan to achieve it, and go to work on your plan immediately. Remember the wonderful words of Goethe: *"Only engage, and the mind grows heated. Begin it, and the work will be completed."*

5 Practice Creative Procrastination

Make time for getting big tasks done every day. Plan your daily workload in advance. Single out the relatively few small jobs that absolutely must be done immediately in the morning. Then go directly to the big tasks and pursue them to completion.

BOARDROOM REPORTS

Creative procrastination is one of the most effective of all personal performance techniques. It can change your life.

The fact is that you can't do everything that you have to do. You have to procrastinate on *something*. Therefore, procrastinate on small tasks. Put off eating smaller or less ugly frogs. Eat the biggest and ugliest frogs before anything else. Do the worst first!

Everyone procrastinates. The difference between high performers and low performers is largely determined by what they choose to procrastinate on.

Since you must procrastinate anyway, decide today to procrastinate on low-value activities. Decide to procrastinate on, outsource, delegate, and eliminate those activities that don't make much of a contribution to your life in any case. Get rid of the tadpoles and focus on the frogs.

Priorities versus Posteriorities

Here is a key point. To set proper priorities, you must set posteriorities as well. A *priority* is something that you do more of and sooner, while a *posteriority* is something that you do less of and later, if at all.

> Rule: You can get your time and your life
> under control only to the degree to which
> you discontinue lower-value activities.

One of the most powerful of all words in time management is the word no! Say it politely. Say it clearly so that there are no misunderstandings. Say it regularly as a normal part of your time management vocabulary.

Say no to anything that is not a high-value use of your time and your life. Say no graciously but firmly to avoid agreeing to something against your will. Say it early and say it often. Remember that you have no spare time. As we say, "Your dance card is full."

For you to do something new, you must complete or stop doing something old. Getting in requires getting out. Picking up means putting down.

Creative procrastination is the act of thoughtfully and deliberately deciding upon the exact things you are not going to do right now, if ever.

Procrastinate on Purpose

Most people engage in *unconscious* procrastination. They procrastinate without thinking about it. As a result, they procrastinate on the big, valuable, important tasks that can have significant long-term consequences in their lives and careers. You must avoid this common tendency at all costs.

Your job is to deliberately procrastinate on tasks that are of low value so that you have more time for tasks that can make a big difference in your life and work. Continually review your duties and responsibilities to identify time-consuming tasks and activities that you can abandon with no real loss. This is an ongoing responsibility for you that never ends.

For example, a friend of mine was an avid golfer when he was single. He liked to golf three or four times a week, three to four hours each time. Over a period of years, he started a business, got married, and had two children. But he still played golf three to four times a week until he finally realized that his time on the golf course was causing him enormous stress at home and at the office. Only by abandoning most of his golf games could he get his life back under control.

Set Posteriorities on Time-Consuming Activities

Continually review your life and work to find time-consuming tasks and activities that you can abandon. Cut down on television watching and instead spend the time with your family, read, exercise, or do something else that enhances the quality of your life.

Look at your work activities and identify the tasks that you could delegate or eliminate to free up more time for the work that really counts. Begin today to practice creative procrastination, to set posteriorities wherever and whenever you can. This decision alone can enable you to get your time and your life under control.

EAT THAT FROG!

1. Practice "zero-based thinking" in every part of your life. Ask yourself continually, "If I were not doing this already, knowing what I now know, would I start doing it again today?" If it is something you would not start again today, knowing what you now know, it is a prime candidate for abandonment or creative procrastination.

2. Examine each of your personal and work activities and evaluate it based on your current situation. Select at least one activity to abandon immediately or at least deliberately put off until your more important goals have been achieved.

6
Use the ABCDE Method Continually

The first law of success is concentration—
to bend all the energies to one point,
and to go directly to that point, looking
neither to the right nor to the left.
WILLIAM MATHEWS

The more thought you invest in planning and setting priorities before you begin, the more important things you will do and the faster you will get them done once you get started. The more important and valuable a task is to you, the more likely you will be motivated to overcome procrastination and launch yourself into the job.

The ABCDE Method is a powerful priority setting technique that you can use every single day. This technique is so simple and effective that it can, all by itself, make you one of the most efficient and effective people in your field.

Think on Paper

The power of this technique lies in its simplicity. Here's how it works: You start with a list of everything you have to do for the coming day. Think on paper.

You then place an *A, B, C, D,* or *E* next to each item on your list before you begin the first task.

An "A" item is defined as something that is very important, something that you must do. This is a task that will have serious positive or negative consequences if you do it or fail to do it, like visiting a key customer or finishing a report that your boss needs for an upcoming board meeting. These items are the frogs of your life.

If you have more than one A task, you prioritize these tasks by writing "A-1," "A-2," "A-3," and so on in front of each item. Your A-1 task is your biggest, ugliest frog of all.

"Shoulds" versus "Musts"

A "B" item is defined as a task that you *should* do. But it has only mild consequences. These are the tadpoles of your work life. This means that someone may be unhappy or inconvenienced if you don't do one of these tasks, but it is nowhere as important as an A task. Returning an unimportant telephone message or reviewing your e-mail would be a B task.

The rule is that you should never do a B task when an A task is left undone. You should never be distracted by a tadpole when a big frog is sitting there waiting to be eaten.

A "C" task is defined as something that would be *nice* to do but for which there are no consequences at all, whether you do it or not. C tasks include phoning a friend, having coffee or lunch with a coworker, and com-

completing some personal business during work hours. These sorts of activities have no affect at all on your work life.

A "D" task is defined as something you can *delegate* to someone else. The rule is that you should delegate everything that someone else can do so that you can free up more time for the A tasks that only you can do.

An "E" task is defined as something that you can *eliminate* altogether, and it won't make any real difference. This may be a task that was important at one time but is no longer relevant to you or anyone else. Often it is something you continue to do out of habit or because you enjoy it. But every minute that you spend on an E task is time taken away from a task or activity that can make a real difference in your life.

After you have applied the ABCDE Method to your list, you will be completely organized and ready to get more important things done faster.

Take Action Immediately

The key to making this ABCDE Method work is for you to now discipline yourself to start immediately on your A-1 task and then stay at it until it is complete. Use your willpower to get going and stay going on this one job, the most important single task you could possibly be doing. Eat the whole frog and don't stop until it's finished completely.

Your ability to think through and analyze your work list and determine your A-1 task is the springboard to higher levels of accomplishment and greater self-esteem, self-respect, and personal pride. When you develop the habit of concentrating on your A-1, most important, activity—on eating your frog—you will start getting more done than any two or three people around you.

EAT THAT FROG!

1. Review your work list right now and put an *A, B, C, D,* or *E* next to each task or activity. Select your A-1 job or project and begin on it immediately. Discipline yourself to do nothing else until this one job is complete.

2. Practice this ABCDE Method every day for the next month on every work or project list before you begin work. After a month, you will have developed the habit of setting and working on your highest-priority tasks, and your future will be assured!

7 Focus on Key Result Areas

When every physical and mental resource
is focused, one's power to solve a problem
multiplies tremendously.

NORMAN VINCENT PEALE

"Why am I on the payroll?" This is one of the most important questions you can ever ask and answer, over and over again, throughout your career.

As it happens, most people are not sure exactly why they are on the payroll. But if you are not crystal clear about why you are on the payroll and what results you have been hired to accomplish, it is very hard for you to perform at your best, get paid more, and get promoted faster.

In simple terms, you have been hired to get specific results. A wage or a salary is a payment for a specific quality and quantity of work that can be combined with the work of others to create a product or service that customers are willing to pay for.

Your job can be broken down into about five to seven key result areas, seldom more. These represent the results that you absolutely, positively have to get to fulfill your responsibilities and make your maximum contribution to your organization.

A key result area is defined as something for which you are completely responsible. If you don't do it, it doesn't get done. A key result area is an activity that is under your control. It produces an output that becomes an input or a contributing factor to the work of others.

Key result areas are similar to the vital functions of the body, such as those indicated by blood pressure, heart rate, respiratory rate, and brain-wave activity. An absence of any one of these vital functions leads to the death of the organism. By the same token, your failure to perform in a critical result area of your work can lead to the end of your job as well.

The Big Seven in Management and Sales

The key result areas of management are planning, organizing, staffing, delegating, supervising, measuring, and reporting. These are the areas in which a manager must get results to succeed in his or her area of responsibility. A weakness in any one of these areas can lead to under-achievement and failure as a manager.

The key result areas of sales are prospecting, building rapport and trust, identifying needs, presenting persuasively, answering objections, closing the sale, and getting resales and referrals. Poor performance in any one of these key skills can lead to lower sales and sometimes the failure of a salesperson.

Whatever you do, you must have certain essential skills for you to do your job in an excellent fashion. These demands are constantly changing. You have developed core competencies that make it possible for you to do your job in the first place. But certain key results are central to your work and determine your success or failure in your job. What are they?

Clarity Is Essential

The starting point of high performance is for you to identify the key result areas of your work. Discuss them with your boss. Make a list of your most important output responsibilities, and make sure that the people above you, on the same level as you, and below you are in agreement with it.

For example, for a salesperson, getting qualified appointments is a key result area. This activity is the key to the entire sales process. Closing a sale is a key result area. When the sale is made, it triggers the activities of many other people to produce and deliver the product or service.

For a company owner or key executive, negotiating a bank loan may be a key result area. Hiring the right people and delegating effectively are both key result areas. For a receptionist or secretary, typing letters and answering the phone and transferring callers quickly and efficiently are defined as key result areas. People's ability to perform these tasks quickly and efficiently largely determines their pay and promotability.

Give Yourself a Grade

Once you have determined your key result areas, the second step is for you to grade yourself on a scale of one to ten (with one being the lowest and ten being the highest) in each of those areas. Where are you strong and where are you weak? Where are you getting excellent results and where are you underperforming?

> Rule: Your *weakest* key result area sets the height
> at which you can use all your other skills and abilities.

This rule says that although you could be exceptional in six out of your seven key result areas, poor performance in the seventh area will hold you back and determine how much you achieve with all your other skills. This weakness will act as a drag on your effectiveness and be a constant source of friction and frustration.

For example, delegating is a key result area for a manager. This skill is the key leverage point that enables a manager to manage, to get results through others. A manager who cannot delegate properly is held back from using all his or her other skills at the maximum levels of effectiveness. Poor delegation skills alone can lead to failure in the job.

Poor Performance Produces Procrastination

One of the major reasons for procrastination in the workplace is that people avoid jobs and activities in those areas where they have performed poorly in the past. Instead of setting a goal and making a plan to improve in a particular area, most people avoid that area altogether, which just makes the situation worse.

The reverse of this is that the *better* you become in a particular skill area, the more motivated you will be to perform that function, the less you will procrastinate, and the more determined you will be to get the job finished.

The fact is that everybody has both strengths and weaknesses. Refuse to rationalize, justify, or defend your areas of weakness. Instead, identify them clearly. Set a goal and make a plan to become very good in each of those areas. Just think! You may be only one critical skill away from top performance at your job.

The Great Question

Here is one of the greatest questions you will ever ask and answer: **"What one skill, if I developed and did it in an excellent fashion, would have the greatest positive impact on my career?"**

You should use this question to guide your career for the rest of your life. Look into yourself for the answer. You probably know what it is.

Ask your boss this question. Ask your coworkers. Ask your friends and your family. Whatever the answer is, find out and then go to work to bring up your performance in this area.

The good news is that all business skills are *learnable*. If anyone else is excellent in that particular key result area, this is proof that you can become excellent as well, if you decide to.

One of the fastest and best ways to stop procrastinating and get more things done faster is for you to become absolutely excellent in your key result areas. This can be as important as anything else you do in your life or your career.

EAT THAT FROG!

1. Identify the key result areas of your work. What are they? Write down the key results you have to get to do your job in an excellent fashion. Give yourself a grade from one to ten on each one. And then determine the one key skill that, if you did it in an excellent manner, would help you the most in your work.

2. Take this list to your boss and discuss it with him or her. Invite honest feedback and appraisal. You can get better only when you are open to the constructive input of other people. Discuss your results with your staff and coworkers. Talk them over with your spouse.

Make a habit of doing this analysis regularly for the rest of your career. Never stop improving. This decision alone can change your life.

8
Apply the Law of Three

Do what you can, with what you have,
where you are.

THEODORE ROOSEVELT

Three core tasks that you perform contain most of the value that you contribute to your business or organization. Your ability to accurately identify these three key tasks and then to focus on them most of the time is essential for you to perform at your best. Let me tell you a true story.

Three months after her first full-day coaching session with me in San Diego, Cynthia stood up and told the group a story. She said, "When I came here ninety days ago, you claimed that you would show me how to double my income and double my time off within twelve months. This sounded completely unrealistic, but I was willing to give it a try.

"On the first day, you asked me to write down a list of everything that I did over the course of a week or a month. I came up with seventeen tasks that I was responsible for. My problem was that I was completely overwhelmed with work. I was working ten to twelve hours per day, six days per week, and not spending enough time with my husband and my two young children. But I didn't see any way out.

"I had been working for eight years for a fast-growing entrepreneurial company in the high-tech area, but there always seemed to be an overwhelming amount of work to do and never enough time."

One Thing All Day Long

She continued with her story. "Once I had made up this list, you then told me to ask this question: 'If you could do only one thing on this list all day long, which one task would contribute the greatest value to your company?' Once I had identified that task, which was quite easy, I put a circle around that number.

"You then asked, 'If you could do only one more thing on your list of key tasks, which would be the *second* activity that contributes the most value to your company?'

"Once I had identified the second most important task, you asked me the same question with regard to the *third* most important task.

"You then said something that shocked me at the time. You said that fully 90 percent of the value that you contribute to your company is contained in those three tasks, whatever they are. Everything else you do is either a support task or a complementary task that could probably be delegated, downsized, outsourced, or eliminated."

Take Immediate Action

Cynthia continued with her story. "As I looked at the three tasks, I realized that these were the three things that I did that contributed the most value to my company. This was on a Friday. On Monday morning at 10 o'clock, I met with my boss and explained to him what I had discovered. I told him that I needed his help in delegating and outsourcing all my work except for those three key tasks. I felt that if I could work on those three tasks exclusively, all day long, I could more than double my contribution to the company. Then I said to him that if I doubled my contribution, I would like to be paid twice as much."

She said, "My boss was completely silent. He looked at my list of key tasks, looked back up at me, looked at the list again, and then said, 'Okay.' It was now 10:21 a.m. according to the clock on the wall behind him.

"He said, 'You're right. These are the three most important things that you do in this company—and the three things that you do the best. I will help you to delegate and downsize all these other minor tasks to free you up to work full-time on these three key tasks. And if you double your contribution, I will pay you twice as much.'"

Transform Your Life

Cynthia concluded her story by saying, "He did; then I did; then he did. He helped me delegate and assign my minor tasks so I could concentrate on my top three jobs. As a result, I doubled my output over the next thirty days, and he doubled my income.

"I had been working very hard for more than eight years, and I doubled my income in just one month by focusing all my time and energy on my three key tasks. Not only that, but instead of working ten and twelve hour days, I work from 8:00 to 5:00 and spend time in the evenings and on the weekends with my husband and my children. Focusing on my key tasks has transformed my life."

Perhaps the most important word in the world of work is *contribution*. Your rewards, both financial and emotional, will always be in direct proportion to your results, to the value of your contribution. If you want to increase your rewards, you must focus on increasing the value of what you do. You must dedicate yourself to contributing more results to your company. And three key tasks always contribute the most.

The Quick List Method

Here is an exercise that we use with our coaching clients very early in the process. We give them a sheet of paper and then tell them, "In thirty seconds, write down your three most important goals in life right now."

We have found that when people have only thirty seconds to write their three most important goals, their answers are as accurate as if they had thirty minutes or three hours. Their subconscious minds seem to go into a form of "hyperdrive," and their three most important goals pop out of their heads and onto the paper, often to the surprise of the people doing the exercise.

In 80 percent or more of cases, people have three goals in common: first, a financial and career goal; second, a family or personal relationship goal; and third, a health or a fitness goal. And this is as it should be. These are the three most important areas of life. If you give yourself a grade on a scale of one to ten in each of these three areas, you can immediately identify where you are doing well in life and where you need some improvement. Try it yourself and see. Give this exercise to your spouse or your children. The answers can be quite revealing.

Later in our coaching program, we expand this exercise by asking the following questions:

1. What are your three most important *business or career* goals right now?
2. What are your three most important *family or relationship* goals right now?
3. What are your three most important *financial* goals right now?
4. What are your three most important *health* goals right now?
5. What are your three most important *personal and professional development* goals right now?
6. What are your three most important *social and community* goals right now?
7. What are your three biggest *problems or concerns* in life right now?

When you force yourself to ask and answer each of these questions in thirty seconds or less, you will often be amazed at the answers. Whatever your answers, they will usually be an accurate snapshot of your true situation in life at the moment. These answers will tell you what is really important to you.

While you are setting goals and priorities, getting organized, concentrating single-mindedly on one task at a time, and disciplining yourself to complete your most important tasks, you must never forget that your ultimate goal is to live a long, happy, and healthy life.

Time Management Is a Means to an End

The main reason to develop time management skills is so that you can complete everything that is really important in your work and free up more and more time to do the things in your personal life that give you the greatest happiness and satisfaction.

Fully 85 percent of your happiness in life will come from happy relationships with other people, especially those closest to you, as well as the members of your family. The critical determinant of the quality of your relationships is the amount of time that you spend face-to-face with the people you love, and who love you in return.

The purpose of time management—of eating that frog—and getting more done in less time is to enable you to spend more "face time" with the people you care about, doing the things that give you the greatest amount of joy in life.

Rule: It is the *quality* of time at work that counts and the *quantity* of time at home that matters.

Work All the Time You Work

To keep your life in balance, you should resolve to work all the time you work. When you go to work, put your head down and work the whole time. Start a little earlier, stay a little later, and work a little harder. Don't waste time. Every minute that you spend in idle chitchat with coworkers is time taken away from the work that you must accomplish if you want to keep your job.

Even worse, time that you waste at work often has to be taken away from the members of your family. You have to either stay late or take work home and work in the evenings. By not working effectively and efficiently during your workday, you create unnecessary stress and deprive the members of your family of the very best person you can possibly be.

There is a story of a little girl who goes to her mother and asks, "Mommy, why does Daddy bring a briefcase full of work home each night and never spend any time with the family?" The mother replies sympathetically, "Well, honey, you have to understand—Daddy can't get his work done at the office so he has to bring it home and get caught up here." The little girl then asks, "If that's the case, why don't they put him in a slower class?"

Balance Is Not Optional

One of the most famous sayings of the ancient Greeks was "Moderation in all things." You need balance between your work and your personal life. You need to set priorities at work and concentrate on your most valuable tasks. At the same time, you must never lose sight of the fact that the reason for working efficiently is so that you can enjoy a higher quality of life at home with your family.

Sometimes people come up to me and ask, "How do I achieve balance between my work and my home life?"

I ask them in return, "How often does a tightrope walker balance when on the high wire?" After a few seconds of thinking, they almost always say, "All the time." I say, "That is the same situation with balance between work and home life. You have to do it all the time. You never reach a point where you have attained it perfectly. You have to work at it."

Your goal should be to perform at your very best at work—to get the very most done and enjoy the very highest level of rewards possible for you in your career. Simultaneously, you must always remember to "smell the flowers along the way." Never lose sight of the real reasons why you work as hard as you do and why you are so determined to accomplish the very most with the time that you invest. The more time you spend face-to-face with the people you love, the happier you will be.

EAT THAT FROG!

1. Determine the three most important tasks that you do in your work. Ask yourself, "If I could do only one thing all day long, which one task would contribute the greatest value to my career?" Do this exercise two more times. Once you have identified your "big three," concentrate on them single-mindedly all day long.

2. Identify your three most important goals in each area of your life. Organize them by priority. Make plans for their accomplishment, and work on your plans every single day. You will be amazed at what you achieve in the months and years ahead.

9
Prepare Thoroughly Before You Begin

No matter what the level of your ability,
you have more potential than you can
ever develop in a lifetime.

JAMES T. McCAY

One of the best ways for you to overcome procrastination and get more things done faster is to have everything you need at hand before you begin. When you are fully prepared, you are like a cocked gun or an archer with an arrow pulled back taut in the bow. You will be amazed at what you achieve in the months and years ahead. You just need one small mental push to get started on your highest value tasks.

This is like getting everything ready to prepare a complete meal, such as a big frog. You set all the ingredients out on the counter in front of you and then begin putting the meal together, one step at a time.

Begin by clearing off your desk or workspace so that you have only one task in front of you. If necessary, put everything on the floor or on a table behind you. Gather all the information, reports, details, papers, and work materials that you will require to complete the job. Have them at hand so you can reach them without getting up or moving much.

Be sure that you have all the writing materials, computer disks, access codes, e-mail addresses, and everything else you need to start working and continue working until the job is done.

Set up your work area so that it is comfortable, attractive, and conducive to working for long periods. Especially, make sure that you have a comfortable chair that supports your back and allows your feet to rest flat on the floor.

Create a Comfortable Workspace

The most productive people take the time to create a work area where they enjoy spending time. The cleaner and neater your work area before you begin, the easier it will be for you to get started and keep going.

One of the great techniques for overcoming procrastination (eating frogs) is for you to get everything that you need to work completely ready, in advance. When everything is laid out neatly and in sequence, you will feel much more like getting on with the job.

Get On with the Job

It is amazing how many books never get written, how many degrees never get completed, how many life-changing tasks never get started because people fail to take the first step of preparing everything in advance.

Los Angeles attracts people from all over America who dream of writing a successful movie script and selling it to one of the studios. They move to Los Angeles and work at low-level jobs for years while they dream of writing and selling a popular script.

The *Los Angeles Times* once sent a reporter out onto Wilshire Boulevard to interview passersby. When people came along, he asked them one question: "How is your script coming?" Three out of four passersby replied, "Almost done!"

The sad fact is that "almost done" probably meant "not yet started." Don't let this happen to you.

Launch toward Your Dreams

Once you have completed your preparations, it is essential that you launch immediately toward your goals. Get started. Do the first thing, whatever it is.

My personal rule is "Get it 80 percent right and then correct it later." Run it up the flagpole and see if anyone salutes. Don't expect perfection the first time or even the first few times. Be prepared to fail over and over before you get it right.

The biggest enemies we have to overcome on the road to success are not a lack of ability and a lack of opportunity but fears of failure and rejection and the doubts that they trigger. The only way to overcome your fears is to "do the thing you fear," as Emerson wrote, "and the death of fear is certain."

Wayne Gretzky, the great hockey player, once said, "You miss 100 percent of the shots you don't take." Once you have completed your preparations, have the courage to take the first action, and everything else will follow from that. The way you develop the courage you need is to act as if you already had the courage and behave accordingly.

Take the First Step

When you sit down with everything in front of you, ready to go, assume the body language of high performance. Sit up straight; sit forward and away from the back of the chair. Carry yourself as though you were an efficient, effective, high-performing personality. Then, pick up the first item and say to yourself, "Let's get to work!" and plunge in. And once you've started, keep going until the job is finished.

EAT THAT FROG!

1. Take a good look at your desk or office, both at home and at the office. Ask yourself, "What kind of a person works in an environment like that?" The cleaner and neater your work environment, the more positive, productive, and confident you feel.

2. Resolve today to clean up your desk and office completely so that you feel effective, efficient, and ready to get going each time you sit down to work.

10

Take It One Oil Barrel at a Time

Persons with comparatively moderate powers
will accomplish much, if they apply themselves
wholly and indefatigably to one thing at a time.
SAMUEL SMILES

There is an old saying that "by the yard it's hard; but
inch by inch, anything's a cinch!"

One of the best ways to overcome procrastination is
for you to get your mind off the huge task in front of you
and focus on a single action that you can take. One of
the best ways to eat a large frog is for you to take it one
bite at a time.

Lao-tzu wrote, "A journey of a thousand leagues begins with a single step." This is a great strategy for overcoming procrastination and getting more things done
faster.

Crossing a Great Desert

Many years ago, driving an old Land Rover, I crossed
the heart of the Sahara Desert, the Tanezrouft, deep in
modern-day Algeria. By that time, the desert had been

abandoned by the French for years, and the original re-fueling stations were empty and shuttered.

The desert was 500 miles across in a single stretch, without water, food, a blade of grass, or even a fly. It was totally flat, like a broad, yellow sand parking lot that stretched to the horizon in all directions.

More than 1,300 people had perished in the crossing of that stretch of the Sahara in previous years. Often, drifting sands had obliterated the track across the desert, and the travelers had gotten lost in the night, never to be found again alive.

To counter this lack of features in the terrain, the French had marked the track with black, fifty-five-gallon oil drums every five kilometers, which was exactly the distance to the horizon, formed by the curvature of the earth.

Because of this, in the daytime, we could see two oil barrels—the one we had just passed and the one five kilometers ahead of it. And that was all we needed to stay on course.

All we had to do was to steer for the next oil barrel. As a result, we were able to cross the biggest desert in the world by simply taking it "one oil barrel at a time."

Take It One Step at a Time

In the same way, you can accomplish the biggest task in your life by disciplining yourself to take it just one step at a time. Your job is to go as far as you can see. You will then see far enough to go further.

To accomplish a great task, you must step out in faith and have complete confidence that your next step will soon become clear to you. Remember this wonderful advice: "Leap—and the net will appear!"

A great life or a great career is built by performing one task at a time, quickly and well, and then going on to the next task. Financial independence is achieved by saving a little money every single month, year after year. Health and fitness are accomplished by just eating a little less and exercising a little more, day after day and month after month.

You can overcome procrastination and accomplish extraordinary things by taking just the first step, getting started toward your goal, and then taking it one step, one oil barrel, at a time.

EAT THAT FROG!

1. Select any goal, task, or project in your life on which you have been procrastinating and make a list of all the steps you will need to take to eventually complete the task.

2. Then take just one step immediately. Sometimes all you need to do to get started is to sit down and complete one item on the list. And then do one more, and so on. You will be amazed at what you eventually accomplish.

11

Upgrade Your Key Skills

The only certain means of success is to render more and better service than is expected of you, no matter what your task may be.

OG MANDINO

Upgrading your skills is one of the most important personal productivity principles of all. Learn what you need to learn so that you can do your work in an excellent fashion. The better you become at eating a particular type of frog, the more likely you are to just plunge in and get it done.

A major reason for procrastination is a feeling of inadequacy, a lack of confidence, or an inability in a key area of a task. Feeling weak or deficient in a single area is enough to discourage you from starting the job at all.

Continually upgrade your skills in your key result areas. Remember, however good you are today, your knowledge and skills are becoming obsolete at a rapid rate. As Pat Riley, the basketball coach, said, "Anytime you stop striving to get better, you're bound to get worse."

Never Stop Learning

One of the most helpful of all time management techniques is for you to get *better* at your key tasks. Personal and professional improvement is one of the best time savers there is. The better you are at a key task, the more motivated you are to launch into it. The better you are, the more energy and enthusiasm you have. When you know that you can do a job well, you find it easier to overcome procrastination and get the job done faster and better than under any other circumstances.

One piece of information or one additional skill can make an enormous difference in your ability to do the job well. Identify the most important things you do, and then make a plan to continually upgrade your skills in those areas.

> Rule: Continuous learning is the minimum
> requirement for success in any field.

Refuse to allow a weakness or a lack of ability in any area to hold you back. Everything is learnable. And what others have learned, you can learn as well.

When I began to write my first book, I was discouraged because I could use only the hunt-and-peck method of typing. I soon realized that I had to learn to touch-type if I was ever going to write and rewrite a 300-page book. So I bought a touch-typing program for my computer and practiced for twenty to thirty minutes every day for three months. By the end of that time, I was typing forty to fifty words per minute. With this additional skill, I have been able to write more than forty books that have now been published all over the world.

The best news is that you can learn whatever skills you need to be more productive and more effective. You can become a touch typist if necessary. You can become proficient with a computer. You can become a terrific negotiator or a super salesperson. You can learn to speak in public. You can learn to write effectively and well. These are all skills you can acquire as soon as you decide to and make them a priority.

Three Steps to Mastery

First, read in your field for at least one hour every day. Get up a little earlier in the morning and read for thirty to sixty minutes in a book or magazine that contains information that can help you to be more effective and productive at what you do.

Second, take every course and seminar available on the key skills that can help you. Attend the conventions and business meetings of your profession or occupation. Go to the sessions and workshops. Sit up front and take notes. Purchase the audio recordings of the programs. Dedicate yourself to becoming one of the most knowledgeable and competent people in your field.

Third, listen to audio programs in your car. The average car owner sits behind the wheel 500 to 1,000 hours each year while driving from place to place. Turn driving time into learning time. You can become one of the smartest, most capable, and highest paid people in your field simply by listening to educational audio programs as you drive around.

The more you learn and know, the more confident and motivated you feel. The better you become, the more capable you will be of doing even more in your field.

The more you learn, the more you can learn. Just as you can build your physical muscles through physical exercise, you can build your mental muscles with mental exercises. And there is no limit to how far or how fast you can advance except for the limits you place on your own imagination.

EAT THAT FROG!

1. Resolve today to become a "do-it-to-yourself" project. Become a lifelong student of your craft. School is never out for the professional.

2. Identify the key skills that can help you the most to achieve better and faster results. Determine the core competencies that you will need to have in the future to lead your field. Whatever they are, set a goal, make a plan, and begin developing and increasing your ability in those areas. Decide to be the very best at what you do!

12

Leverage Your
Special Talents

Do your work; not just your work and no more,
but a little more for the lavishing's sake—that
little more which is worth all the rest.

DEAN BRIGGS

You are remarkable! You have special talents and abilities that make you different from every other person who has ever lived. There are frogs you can eat, or learn to eat, that can make you one of the most important people in your business or organization.

There are certain things that you can do, or learn to do, that can make you extraordinarily valuable to yourself and to others. Your job is to identify your special areas of uniqueness and then to commit yourself to becoming very, very good in those areas.

Increase Your Earning Ability

Your most valuable asset in terms of cash flow is your earning ability. Your ability to work enables you to bring tens of thousands of dollars into your life every year by simply applying your knowledge and skills to your world. This is your ability to eat specific frogs faster and better than others.

You could lose everything you own—your house, your car, your job, your bank account—but as long as you still had your earning ability, you could make it all back and more besides.

Take stock of your unique talents and abilities on a regular basis. What is it that you do especially well? What are you good at? What do you do easily and well that is difficult for other people? Looking back at your career, what has been most responsible for your success in life and work to date? What have been the most significant frogs you have eaten in the past?

Do What You Love to Do

You are designed such that you will most enjoy doing the very things that you can be the very best at. What is it that you enjoy the most about your work? What kind of frogs do you most enjoy eating? The very fact that you enjoy something means that you probably have within yourself the capability to be excellent in that area.

One of your great responsibilities in life is for you to decide for yourself what you really love to do and then to throw your whole heart into doing that special thing very, very well.

Look at your various tasks and responsibilities. What is it that you do that gets you the most compliments and praise from other people? What do you do that positively affects the work and performance of other people more than anything else?

Successful people are invariably those who have taken the time to identify what they do well and most enjoy. They know what they do that really makes a difference in their work, and they then concentrate on that task or area of activity exclusively.

You should always focus your best energies and abilities on starting and completing those key tasks that your unique talents and abilities enable you to do well and that make a significant contribution. You cannot do everything, but you can do those few things in which you excel, the few things that can really make a difference.

EAT THAT FROG!

1. Continually ask yourself these key questions: "What am I really good at? What do I enjoy the most about my work? What has been most responsible for my success in the past? If I could do any job at all, what job would it be?"

If you won the lottery or came into an enormous amount of money and you could choose any job or any part of a job to do for the indefinite future, what work would you choose?

2. Develop a personal plan to prepare yourself to do your most important tasks in an excellent fashion. Focus on those areas where you have special talents and that you most enjoy. This is the key to unlocking your personal potential.

13
Identify Your
Key Constraints

Concentrate all your thoughts on the
task at hand. The sun's rays do not burn
until brought to a focus.

ALEXANDER GRAHAM BELL

Between where you are today and any goal or objective
that you want to accomplish, there is one major constraint that must be overcome before you can achieve
that major goal. Your job is to identify it clearly.

What is holding you back? What sets the speed at
which you achieve your goals? What determines how
fast you move from where you are to where you want to
go? What stops you or holds you back from eating the
frogs that can really make a difference? Why aren't you
at your goal already?

These are some of the most important questions you
will ever ask and answer on your way to achieving high
levels of personal productivity and effectiveness. Whatever you have to do, there is always a *limiting factor* that
determines how quickly and well you get it done. Your
job is to study the task and identify the limiting factor or

constraint within it. You must then focus all of your energies on alleviating that single choke point.

Identify the Limiting Factor

In virtually every task, large or small, a single factor sets the speed at which you achieve the goal or complete the job. What is it? Concentrate your mental energies on that one key area. This can be the most productive use of your time and talents.

This constraint may be a person whose help or decision you need, a resource that you require, a weakness in some part of the organization, or something else. But the limiting factor is always there, and it is always your job to find it.

For example, the purpose of a business is to create and keep customers. By doing this in sufficient quantities, the company makes a profit and continues to grow and flourish.

Every business has a limiting factor or choke point that determines how quickly and well the company achieves this purpose. It may be the marketing, the level of sales, or the sales force itself. It may be the costs of operation or the methods of production. It may be the level of cash flow or costs. The success of the company may be determined by the competition, the customers, or the current marketplace. One of these factors, more than anything else, determines how quickly the company achieves its goals of growth and profitability. What is it?

The accurate identification of the limiting factor in any process and the focus on that factor can usually bring about more progress in a shorter period than any other single activity.

The 80/20 Rule Applied to Constraints

The 80/20 Rule also applies to the constraints in your life and in your work. This means that 80 percent of the constraints, the factors that are holding you back from achieving your goals, are *internal*. They are within yourself—within your own personal qualities, abilities, habits, disciplines, or competencies. Or they are contained within your own company or organization.

Only 20 percent of the limiting factors are *external* to you or to your organization. Only 20 percent are on the outside in the form of competition, markets, governments, or other organizations.

Your key constraint can be something small and not particularly obvious. Sometimes you have to make a list of every step in a process and examine every activity to determine exactly what is holding you back. Sometimes a single negative perception or objection on the part of customers can be slowing down the entire sales process. Sometimes the absence of a single feature can be holding back the growth of sales of a product or service line.

Look into your company honestly. Look within your boss, your coworkers, and members of your staff to see if there is a key weakness that is holding you or the company back, acting as a brake on the achievement of your key goals.

Look into Yourself

Successful people always begin the analysis of constraints by asking the question, "What is it *in me* that is holding me back?" They accept complete responsibility for their lives and look to themselves for both the cause and cure of their problems.

In your own life, you must have the honesty to look deeply into yourself for the limiting factor or limiting skill that sets the speed at which you achieve your own personal goals. Keep asking, "What sets the speed at which I get the results I want?"

Strive for Accuracy

The definition of the constraint determines the strategy that you use to alleviate it. The failure to identify the correct constraint, or the identification of the wrong constraint, can lead you off in the wrong direction. You can end up solving the wrong problem.

A major corporation, a client of mine, was experiencing declining sales. The corporation's leaders concluded that the major constraint was the quality of the sales force and the sales management. They spent an enormous amount of money reorganizing the management and retraining the salespeople.

They later found that the primary reason that sales were down was a mistake made by an accountant who had accidentally priced their products too high relative to their competition in the marketplace. Once the corporation revamped its pricing, its sales went back up and it returned to profitability.

Behind every constraint or choke point, once it is located and alleviated successfully, you will find another constraint or limiting factor. Whether you're trying to get to work on time in the morning or build a successful career, there are always limiting factors and bottlenecks that set the speed of your progress. Your job is to find them and to focus your energies on alleviating them as quickly as possible.

Starting off your day with the removal of a key bottleneck or constraint fills you full of energy and personal power. It propels you into following through and completing the job. And there is always something. Often, alleviating a key constraint or limiting factor is the most important frog you could eat at that moment.

EAT THAT FROG!

1. Identify your most important goal in life today. What is it? What one goal, if you achieved it, would have the greatest positive effect on your life? What one career accomplishment would have the greatest positive impact on your work life?

2. Determine the one constraint, internal or external, that sets the speed at which you accomplish this goal. Ask, "Why haven't I reached it already? What is it in me that is holding me back?" Whatever your answers, take action immediately. Do something. Do anything, but get started.

14 Put the Pressure on Yourself

The first requisite for success is the ability
to apply your physical and mental energies to
one problem incessantly without growing weary.
THOMAS EDISON

The world is full of people who are waiting for someone
to come along and motivate them to be the kind of people they wish they could be. The problem is that no one
is coming to the rescue.

These people are waiting for a bus on a street where
no buses pass. If they don't take charge of their lives and
put the pressure on themselves, they can end up waiting
forever. And that is what most people do.

Only about 2 percent of people can work entirely
without supervision. We call these people "leaders." This
is the kind of person you are meant to be and that you
can be, it you decide to be.

To reach your full potential, you must form the habit
of putting the pressure on yourself and not waiting for
someone else to come along and do it for you. You must
choose your own frogs and then make yourself eat them
in their order of importance.

Lead the Field

See yourself as a role model for others. Raise the bar on yourself. The standards you set for your own work and behavior should be higher than anyone else could set for you.

Make it a game with yourself to start a little earlier, work a little harder, and stay a little later. Always look for ways to go the extra mile, to do more than you are paid for.

Your self-esteem, the core of your personality, has been defined by psychologist Nathaniel Branden as "the reputation you have with yourself." You build up or pull down your reputation with yourself with everything you do or fail to do. The good news is that you feel better about yourself whenever you push yourself to do your best. You increase your self-esteem whenever you go beyond the point where the average person would normally quit.

Create Imaginary Deadlines

One of the best ways for you to overcome procrastination is by working as though you had only one day to get your most important jobs done.

Imagine each day that you have just received an emergency message and that you will have to leave town tomorrow for a month. If you had to leave town for a month, what would you make absolutely sure that you got done before you left? Whatever your answer, go to work on that task right now.

Another way to put pressure on yourself is to imagine that you just received an all-expenses-paid one-week vacation at a beautiful resort as a prize, but you will have to leave tomorrow morning on the vacation or it will be given to someone else. What would you be determined to get finished before you left so that you could take that vacation? Whatever it is, start on that one job immediately.

Successful people continually put the pressure on themselves to perform at high levels. Unsuccessful people have to be instructed and supervised and pressured by others.

By putting the pressure on yourself, you will accomplish more and better tasks faster than ever before. You will become a high-performance, high-achieving personality. You will feel terrific about yourself, and bit by bit, you will build up the habit of rapid task completion that will then go on to serve you all the days of your life.

EAT THAT FROG!

1. Set deadlines and subdeadlines on every task and activity. Create your own "forcing system." Raise the bar on yourself and don't let yourself off the hook. Once you've set yourself a deadline, stick to it and even try to beat it.

2. Write out every step of a major job or project before you begin. Determine how many minutes and hours you will require to complete each phase. Then race against your own clock. Beat your own deadlines. Make it a game and resolve to win!

15

Maximize Your Personal Powers

Gather in your resources, rally all your faculties, marshal all your energies, focus all your capacities upon mastery of at least one field of endeavor.
JOHN HAGGAI

The raw material of personal performance and productivity is contained in your physical, mental, and emotional energies. Your body is like a machine that uses food, water, and rest to generate energy that you then use to accomplish important tasks in your life and work. When you are fully rested, for example, you can get two times, three times, and five times as much done as when you are tired or burned out.

One of the most important requirements for being happy and productive is for you to guard and nurture your energy levels at all times.

Overworking Can Mean Underproducing

The fact is that your productivity begins to decline after eight or nine hours of work. For this reason, working long hours into the night, although it is sometimes necessary, means that you are usually producing less and less in more and more time.

The more tired you become, the worse the quality of your work will be and the more mistakes you will make. At a certain point, you can reach "the wall" and simply be unable to continue, like a battery that is run down.

Work at Your Own Pace

There are specific times during the day when you are at your best. You need to identify these times and discipline yourself to use them on your most important and challenging tasks.

Most people are at their best in the morning, after a good night's sleep. Some people are better in the afternoon. A few people are most creative and productive in the evening or late at night.

A major reason for procrastination is fatigue or attempting to start on a task when you are tired. You have no energy or enthusiasm. Like a cold engine in the morning, you can't seem to get yourself started.

Whenever you feel overtired and overwhelmed with too much to do and too little time, stop yourself and just say, "All I can do is all I can do."

Sometimes the very best use of your time is to go home early and go to bed and sleep for ten hours straight. This can completely recharge you and enable you to get two or three times as much work done the following day, and of a far higher quality, than if you had continued working long into the night.

Get Enough Sleep

According to many researchers, the average American is not getting enough sleep relative to the amount of work he or she is doing. Millions of Americans are working in a mental fog as the result of working too much and sleeping too little.

One of the smartest things you can do is to turn off the television and get to bed by 10:00 p.m. each night during the week. Sometimes one extra hour of sleep per night can change your entire life.

Here is a rule for you. Take one full day off every week. During this day, either Saturday or Sunday, absolutely refuse to read, clear correspondence, catch up on things from the office, or do anything else that taxes your brain. Instead, go to a movie, exercise, spend time with your family, go for a walk, or participate in any activity that allows your brain to completely recharge itself. It is true that "a change is as good as a rest."

Take regular vacations each year, both long weekends and one- and two-week breaks to rest and rejuvenate. You are always the most productive after a restful weekend or a vacation.

Going to bed early five nights a week, sleeping in on the weekends, and taking one full day off each week will ensure that you have far more energy. This added energy will enable you to overcome procrastination and get started on your major tasks faster and with greater resolve than you ever could if you were tired.

Guard Your Physical Health

In addition to getting lots of rest, to keep your energy levels at their highest, be careful about what you eat. Start the day with a high-protein, low-fat, and low-carbohydrate breakfast. Eat salads with fish or chicken at lunch. Avoid sugar, salt, white-flour products, and desserts. Avoid soft drinks, candy bars, and pastries. Feed yourself as you would feed a world-class athlete before a competition because in many respects, that's what you are before starting work each day.

Aim to exercise about 200 minutes each week, the agreed-upon standard for excellent levels of fitness. This is equal to about thirty minutes per day and can be achieved by going for a walk before or after work or by walking short stretches during the day. You can swim, use exercise equipment, or play sports, but build exercise into your daily routine, just as if it were a business appointment.

By eating lean and healthy, exercising regularly, and getting lots of rest, you'll get more and better work done easier and with greater satisfaction than ever before.

The better you feel when you start work, the less you will procrastinate and the more eager you will be to get the job done and get on with other tasks. High energy levels are indispensable to higher levels of productivity, more happiness, and greater success in everything you do.

EAT THAT FROG!

1. Analyze your current energy levels and your daily health habits. Resolve today to improve your levels of health and energy by asking the following questions:

What am I doing physically that I should do *more* of?

What am I doing that I should do *less* of?

What am I not doing that I should *start doing* if I want to perform at my best?

What am I doing today that affects my health that I should *stop doing* altogether?

2. Select one activity or behavior that you can change immediately to improve your overall levels of health and energy. Practice that one action over and over until it becomes a habit. Then select a second way to improve and begin on that.

Whatever your answers are to the above questions, take action today.

16
Motivate Yourself into Action

It is in the compelling zest of high adventure and of victory, and of creative action that man finds his supreme joys.

ANTOINE DE SAINT-EXUPÉRY

To perform at your best, you must become your own personal cheerleader. You must develop a routine of coaching yourself and encouraging yourself to play at the top of your game.

Most of your emotions, positive or negative, are determined by how you talk to yourself on a minute-to-minute basis. It is not what happens to you but the way that you interpret the things that are happening to you that determines how you feel. Your version of events largely determines whether these events motivate or demotivate you, whether they energize or deenergize you.

To keep yourself motivated, you must resolve to become a complete optimist. You must decide to respond positively to the words, actions, and reactions of the people and situations around you. You must refuse to let the unavoidable difficulties and setbacks of daily life affect your mood or emotions.

Control Your Inner Dialogue

Your level of self-esteem, how much you like and respect yourself, is central to your levels of motivation and persistence. You should talk to yourself positively all the time to boost your self-esteem. Say things like "I like myself! I like myself!" over and over until you begin to believe it and behave like a person with a high-performance personality.

To keep yourself motivated and to overcome feelings of doubt or fear, continually tell yourself, "I can do it! I can do it!" When people ask you how you are, always tell them, "I feel terrific!"

No matter how you really feel at the moment or what is happening in your life, resolve to remain cheerful and upbeat. As Viktor Frankl wrote in his bestselling book *Man's Search for Meaning,* "The last of the human freedoms [is] to choose one's attitude in any given set of cricumstances."

Refuse to complain about your problems. Keep them to yourself. As speaker-humorist Ed Foreman says, "You should never share your problems with others because 80 percent of people don't care about them anyway, and the other 20 percent are kind of glad that you've got them in the first place."

Develop a Positive Mental Attitude

In Martin Seligman's twenty-two-year study at the University of Pennsylvania, summarized in his book *Learned*

Optimism, he determined that optimism is the most important quality you can develop for personal and professional success and happiness. Optimistic people seem to be more effective in almost every area of life.

It turns out that optimists have four special behaviors, all learned through practice and repetition. First, optimists *look for the good* in every situation. No matter what goes wrong, they always look for something good or beneficial. And not surprisingly, they always seem to find it.

Second, optimists always *seek the valuable lesson in every setback or difficulty.* They believe that "difficulties come not to obstruct but to instruct." They believe that each setback or obstacle contains a valuable lesson they can learn and grow from, and they are determined to find it.

Third, optimists always *look for the solution to every problem.* Instead of blaming or complaining when things go wrong, they become action oriented. They ask questions like "What's the solution? What can we do now? What's the next step?"

Fourth, optimists *think and talk continually about their goals.* They think about what they want and how to get it. They think and talk about the future and where they are going rather than the past and where they came from. They are always looking forward rather than backward.

When you continually visualize your goals and ideals and talk to yourself in a positive way, you feel more focused and energized. You feel more confident and creative. You experience a greater sense of control and personal power.

And the more positive and motivated you feel, the more eager you are to get started and the more determined you are to keep going.

EAT THAT FROG!

1. Control your thoughts. Remember, you become what you think about most of the time. Be sure that you are thinking and talking about the things you want rather than the things you don't want.

2. Keep your mind positive by accepting complete responsibility for yourself and for everything that happens to you. Refuse to criticize others, complain, or blame others for anything. Resolve to make progress rather than excuses. Keep your thoughts and your energy focused forward, on what you can do right now to improve your life, and let the rest go.

17
Get Out of the Technological Time Sinks

There is more to life than just increasing its speed.

GANDHI

Technology can be your best friend or your worst enemy. As we race into the twenty-first century, bombarded by information from all sides, many people seem to have an irresistible, if not obsessive, need to communicate continually with people everywhere—in their personal and business lives.

This compulsion to communicate incessantly—entailing the nonstop use of cell phones, BlackBerry devices, personal digital assistants, the Internet (both wireless and wired), and various contact management systems such as Microsoft Outlook and Maximizer—tends to leave people psychologically breathless. We have no time to stop, smell the roses, and collect our thoughts.

You Have a Choice

At the same time, many high-powered, hardworking, highly productive people functioning in the dead center of communications technology are not overwhelmed by technology. They seem to have their lives largely under control.

Bill Gross, manager of more than $600 billion in fixed-income funds and bonds, is famous for exercising regularly and meditating daily to keep centered while using no technology at all. He turns off his phones, leaves his BlackBerry in his office, and exercises without the continual interruptions of people who have an overwhelming need to stay connected. And he says that he never misses an important message.

For you to stay calm, clearheaded, and capable of performing at your best, you need to detach on a regular basis from the technology and communication devices that can overwhelm you if you are not careful.

Don't Become Addicted

In Washington not long ago, I was at a business luncheon with a roomful of high-level executives. Prior to the beginning of the luncheon, one of the organizers stood up and said a short grace. Everyone bowed their heads. When the grace was over, the luncheon began.

However, at my table, four or five out of the eight people seemed to have been greatly affected by the prayer. They kept their heads down and their hands in their laps, even when the food was served. They seemed to be lost in deep thought over the profound questions of the day.

Then I realized that they were not praying at all. They were all intensely focused on their BlackBerry devices, sending and receiving e-mail, working their little keyboards like frantic teenagers playing video games. They were all lost to the world around them as they messaged back and forth, some of them with other people in the same room. They had fallen into a technological trap, a deep sink full of information exchange in which they were drowning.

Technology Is Your Friend

The purpose of modern technology is largely to increase the speed, efficiency, and accuracy of the transfer of information of all kinds. Technology is meant to help us improve the quality of our lives by enabling us to accomplish our key tasks and communicate with the key people in our world faster and more efficiently than ever before.

But the use of communications technology can quickly become a form of addiction. People get up in the morning and immediately check to see if they received any phone calls or voice mail messages on their cell phones. They then race to their computers to pull up their e-mail to see if anyone communicated with them overnight. They call the office to find out if anyone has done or said anything in the last few hours that they should know about. They check their Microsoft Outlook calendars, their personal digital assistants, their

BlackBerry devices, and other forms of communications technology every five or six minutes to make sure that they are not missing anything. This has to stop before it gets out of control.

Take Back Your Time

One of my clients, with distributors in nineteen states, found himself bound and chained to his computer, receiving and responding to e-mails several hours each day. The more time he spent at his computer, the fewer of his other important tasks he was able to get done. The stress caused by these undone tasks, building up like an avalanche overhang, started to affect his personality, his health, and his sleeping habits.

We taught him about the 80/20 Rule and how it applied to e-mails. Fully 80 percent of the e-mails that he received were of no value and should not even be opened. They should be deleted immediately.

Of the remaining 20 percent, only 20 percent of those, or 4 percent of his e-mails, actually required an immediate response of some kind. The other 16 percent could be ignored temporarily or transferred to an action folder where they could be dealt with one at a time.

Standardize and Delegate

My client felt that no one else had the ability to sort his e-mails, more than 300 per day, and that he had to do it all himself, no matter how much time it took. We encouraged him to sit down with his secretary and go through his e-mails, showing her which ones were important, which ones were unimportant, and how to deal with the most common questions and requests.

To his surprise, within two hours his secretary knew enough to handle most of his e-mails for him. From then on, she would come in each morning and delete the 80 percent of e-mails that were of no value. She would transfer the essential e-mails requesting personal action by her boss into a separate folder. If there was a question about an e-mail, she would transfer it to a "process" folder for him to look at at his convenience.

At our next meeting, he told me that he had tracked the results of this exercise and calculated that he was now saving twenty-three hours per week that he could spend on eating his frogs and completing his most important tasks. This simple exercise transformed his life, reduced his stress levels, improved his health and energy, and made him a much more relaxed and positive person.

Here is a question for you: How would your life change if you had an extra twenty-three hours each week with which to think, work, plan, talk with key coworkers, or even go for a walk with your spouse?

Refuse to Be a Slave

A journalist for *Fortune* magazine wrote recently that when he arrived back at the office after a two-week vacation, more than 700 e-mails were waiting for him. He realized that it would take him a week to get through them all, during which time he wouldn't be able to tackle any of the projects waiting on his desk.

For the first time in his career, he took a deep breath and punched the Delete All button, erasing those 700 e-mails forever. He then got busy with the projects that were really important to him and his company.

His explanation was simple: "I realized that, just because somebody sends me an e-mail, it does not mean that they own a piece of my life in terms of my having to reply to them, now or ever. In addition, it occurred to me that if the e-mail was really important, the sender would send it again." And that's exactly what happened.

A Servant, Not a Master

For you to be able to concentrate on those few things that make the most difference in your business or personal life, you must discipline yourself to treat technology as a servant, not as a master. Technology is there to help you, not to hinder you. The purpose of technology is to make your life smoother and easier, not to create complexity, confusion, and stress.

One of the best rules for dealing with technology is to just "leave it off." Resist the urge to start turning on communication devices as soon as you wake up in the morning. Leave the radio off. Leave the television off. Leave your cell phone off. Leave your computer off until you have planned and organized your day. Deliberately create zones of silence in your life where no one and nothing can break through and reach you. Maintain your inner calm by forcing yourself to stop on a regular basis and "listen to the silence."

Sometimes, to get more done of *higher* value, you have to stop doing things of lower value. Keep asking yourself, *"What's important here?"* What is important for you to accomplish at work? What is important in your personal life? If you could only do one or two of the activities available to you, which ones would they be?

Continuous Contact Is Not Essential

Remember, when you go away for a day, a week, or a month on vacation or on business and you are out of touch with your communication devices, nothing happens. The world seems to continue revolving whether or not you are in continuous contact with it. Problems get solved, answers get found, work gets done, and life continues to flow along like Old Man River. Very few things are so important that they cannot wait.

People often ask me at my seminars, "But don't you have to keep current with the news by reading newspapers, listening to the radio, and watching television?"

I tell them, "If it is really important, someone will tell you." If something important happens at home, at work, in the country, or in the world, someone else can spend hours following the news for you, and he or she will usually tell you on the first possible occasion.

Many people discontinue newspaper subscriptions, stop watching broadcast news on television, and refuse to listen to the radio. And surprisingly enough, they remain well informed on most important subjects. Someone always keeps them up to date. You should do the same.

EAT THAT FROG!

1. Resolve today to create zones of silence during your day-to-day activities. Turn off all communication devices and technology for one hour in the morning and one hour in the afternoon. You will be amazed at what happens: nothing!

2. Resolve to take one full day off each week during which you do not touch your computer, check your BlackBerry, or make any attempt to keep in touch with the world of technology. At the end of a day without contact, except by voice, your mind will be calm and clear. By giving your mental batteries time to recharge, free from the incessant interruptions of communication, you will be more relaxed, aware, and alert.

18
Slice and Dice the Task

The beginning of a habit is like an invisible
thread, but every time we repeat the act we
strengthen the strand, add to it another filament,
until it becomes a great cable and binds us
irrevocably, thought and act.

ORISON SWETT MARDEN

A major reason for procrastinating on big, important tasks is that they appear so large and formidable when you first approach them.

One technique that you can use to cut a big task down to size is the "salami slice" method of getting work done. With this method, you lay out the task in detail and then resolve to do just *one slice* of the job for the time being, like eating a roll of salami one slice at a time—or like eating an elephant one bite at a time.

Psychologically, you will find it easier to do a single, small piece of a large project than to start on the whole job. Often, once you have started and completed a single part of the job, you will feel like doing just one more slice. Soon, you will find yourself working through the job one part at a time, and before you know it, the job will be completed.

Develop a Compulsion to Closure

An important point to remember is that you have deep within you an "urge to completion," or what is often referred to as a "compulsion to closure." This means that you actually feel happier and more powerful when you start and complete a task of any kind. You satisfy a deep subconscious need to bring finality to a job or project. This sense of completion or closure motivates you to start the next task or project and then to persist toward final completion. This act of completion triggers the release of endorphins in your brain that was mentioned earlier.

And the bigger the task you start and complete, the better and more elated you feel. The bigger the frog you eat, the greater the surge of personal power and energy you experience.

When you start and finish a small piece of a task, you feel motivated to start and finish another part, then another, and so on. Each small step forward energizes you. You soon develop an inner drive that motivates you to carry through to completion. This completion gives you the great feeling of happiness and satisfaction that accompanies any success.

"Swiss Cheese" Your Tasks

Another technique you can use to get yourself going is called the "Swiss cheese" method of working. You use this technique to get yourself into gear by resolving to punch a hole in the task, like a hole in a block of Swiss cheese.

You Swiss cheese a task when you resolve to work for a specific time period on it. This may be as little as five or ten minutes, after which you will stop and do something else. You will just take one bite of your frog and then rest or do something else.

The power of this method is similar to that of the salami slice method. Once you start working, you develop a sense of forward momentum and a feeling of accomplishment. You become energized and enthusiastic. You feel yourself internally motivated and propelled to keep going until the task is complete.

You should try the salami slice or the Swiss cheese method on any task that seems overwhelming when you approach it for the first time. You will be amazed at how helpful each technique is in overcoming procrastination.

I have several friends who have become best-selling authors by simply resolving to write one page or even one paragraph per day until the book was completed. And you can do the same.

EAT THAT FROG!

1. Put the "salami slice" or "Swiss cheese" technique into action immediately to get started on a large, complex, multitask job that you've been putting off.

2. Become action oriented. A common quality of high-performance men and women is that when they hear a good idea, they take action on it immediately. As a result, they learn more, learn faster, and get much better results. Don't delay. Try it today!

19
Create Large Chunks of Time

Nothing can add more power to your life
than concentrating all of your energies on
a limited set of targets.

NIDO QUBEIN

Most of the really important work you do requires large
chunks of unbroken time to complete. Your ability to
carve out and use these blocks of high-value, highly productive time is central to your ability to make a significant contribution to your work and to your life.

Successful salespeople set aside a specific time period
each day to phone prospects. Rather than procrastinating or delaying on a task that they don't particularly like,
they resolve that they will phone for one solid hour—between 10:00 and 11:00 a.m., for example—and they discipline themselves to follow through on their resolution.

Many business executives set aside a specific time
each day to call customers directly to get feedback, to return phone calls, or to answer correspondence. Some
people allocate specific thirty-to-sixty-minute time periods each day for exercise. Many people read great books

fifteen minutes each night before retiring. In this way, over time, they eventually read dozens of the best books ever written.

Schedule Blocks of Time

The key to the success of this method of working in specific time segments is for you to plan your day in advance and schedule a fixed time period for a particular activity or task. Make work appointments with yourself and then discipline yourself to keep them. Set aside thirty-, sixty- and ninety-minute time segments that you use to work on and complete important tasks.

Many highly productive people schedule specific activities in preplanned time slots all day long. These people build their work lives around accomplishing key tasks one at a time. As a result, they become more and more productive and eventually produce two times, three times, and five times as much as the average person.

Use a Time Planner

A time planner, broken down by day, hour, and minute and organized in advance, can be one of the most powerful personal productivity tools of all. It enables you to see where you can consolidate and create blocks of time for concentrated work.

During these working times, turn off the telephone, eliminate all distractions, and work nonstop. One of the best work habits of all is to get up early and work at home in the morning for several hours. You can get three times as much work done at home without interruptions as you ever could in a busy office where you are surrounded by people and bombarded by phone calls.

Make Every Minute Count

When you fly on business, you can create your office in the air by planning your work thoroughly before you depart. When the plane takes off, you can work nonstop for the entire flight. You will be amazed at how much work you can go through when you work steadily in an airplane, without interruptions.

One of the keys to high levels of performance and productivity is to make every minute count. Use travel and transition times, what are often called "gifts of time," to complete small chunks of larger tasks.

Remember, the pyramids were built one block at a time. A great life or a great career is built one task—and often, one part of a task—at a time. Your job in time management is to deliberately and creatively organize the concentrated time periods you need to get your key jobs done well and on schedule.

EAT THAT FROG!

1. Think continually of different ways that you can save, schedule, and consolidate large chunks of time. Use these times to work on important tasks with the most significant long-term consequences.

2. Make every minute count. Work steadily and continuously without diversion or distraction by planning and preparing your work in advance. Most of all, keep focused on the most important results for which you are responsible.

20
Develop a Sense of Urgency

Do not wait; the time will never be "just right."
Start where you stand, and work with whatever
tools you may have at your command, and
better tools will be found as you go along.
NAPOLEON HILL

Perhaps the most outwardly identifiable quality of high-performing men and women is action orientation. They are in a hurry to get their key tasks completed.

Highly productive people take the time to think, plan, and set priorities. They then launch quickly and strongly toward their goals and objectives. They work steadily, smoothly, and continuously. As a result, they seem to power through enormous amounts of work in the same amount of time that the average person spends socializing, wasting time, and working on low-value activities.

Getting into "Flow"

When you work on your most important tasks at a high and continuous level of activity, you can actually enter into an amazing mental state called "flow." Almost everyone has experienced this at some time. Really successful people are those who get themselves into this state far more often than average.

When you're in the state of flow, which is the highest human state of performance and productivity, something almost miraculous happens to your mind and emotions. You feel elated and clear. Everything you do seems effortless and accurate. You feel happy and energized. You experience a tremendous sense of calm and increased personal effectiveness.

In the state of flow, identified and talked about over the centuries, you actually function on a higher plane of clarity, creativity, and competence. You are more sensitive and aware. Your insight and intuition function with incredible precision. You see the interconnectedness of people and circumstances around you. You often come up with brilliant ideas and insights that enable you to move ahead even more rapidly.

Trigger High Performance in Yourself

One of the ways you can trigger this state of flow is by developing a sense of urgency. This is an inner drive and desire to get on with the job quickly and get it done fast. It is an impatience that motivates you to get going and to keep going. A sense of urgency feels very much like racing against yourself.

With this ingrained sense of urgency, you develop a "bias for action." You take action rather than talking continually about what you are going to do. You focus on specific steps you can take immediately. You concentrate on the things you can do right now to get the results you want and achieve the goals you desire.

A fast tempo seems to go hand in hand with all great success. Developing this tempo requires that you start moving and keep moving at a steady rate. The faster you move, the more impelled you feel to do even more even faster. You enter "the zone."

Build Up a Sense of Momentum

When you regularly take continuous action toward your most important goals, you activate the Momentum Principle of success. This principle says that although it may take tremendous amounts of energy to overcome inertia and get started initially, it then takes far less energy to keep going.

The good news is that the faster you move, the more energy you have. The faster you move, the more you get done and the more effective you feel. The faster you move, the more experience you get and the more you learn. The faster you move, the more competent and capable you become at your work.

A sense of urgency shifts you automatically onto the fast track in your career. The faster you work and the more you get done, the higher will be your levels of self-esteem, self-respect, and personal pride. You feel in complete control of your life and your work.

Do It Now!

One of the simplest and yet most powerful ways to get yourself started is to repeat the words "Do it now! Do it now! Do it now!" over and over to yourself.

If you feel yourself slowing down or becoming distracted by conversations or low-value activities, repeat to yourself the words "Back to work! Back to work! Back to work!" over and over.

In the final analysis, nothing will help you more in your career than for you to get the reputation for being the kind of person who gets important work done quickly and well. This reputation will make you one of the most valuable and respected people in your field.

EAT THAT FROG!

1. Resolve today to develop a sense of urgency in everything you do. Select one area where you have a tendency to procrastinate and make a decision to develop the habit of fast action in that area.

2. When you see an opportunity or a problem, take action on it immediately. When you are given a task or responsibility, take care of it quickly and report back fast. Move rapidly in every important area of your life. You will be amazed at how much better you feel and how much more you get done.

21
Single Handle Every Task

And herein lies the secret of true power.
Learn, by constant practice, how to husband
your resources, and concentrate them,
at any given moment, upon a given point.
JAMES ALLEN

Eat that frog! Every bit of planning, prioritizing, and organizing comes down to this simple concept.

Every great achievement of humankind has been preceded by a long period of hard, concentrated work until the job was done. Your ability to select your most important task, to begin it, and then to concentrate on it single-mindedly until it is complete is the key to high levels of performance and personal productivity.

Once You Get Going, Keep Going

Single handling requires that once you begin, you keep working at the task without diversion or distraction until the job is 100 percent complete. You keep urging yourself onward by repeating the words "Back to work!" over and over whenever you are tempted to stop or do something else.

By concentrating single-mindedly on your most important task, you can reduce the time required to complete it by 50 percent or more.

It has been estimated that the tendency to start and stop a task—to pick it up, put it down, and come back to it—can increase the time necessary to complete the task by as much as 500 percent. Each time you return to the task, you have to familiarize yourself with where you were when you stopped and what you still have to do. You have to overcome inertia and get yourself going again. You have to develop momentum and get into a productive work rhythm.

But when you prepare thoroughly and then begin, refusing to stop or turn aside until the job is done, you develop energy, enthusiasm, and motivation. You get better and better and more productive. You work faster and more effectively.

Don't Waste Time

The truth is that once you have decided on your number one task, anything else that you do other than that is a relative waste of time. Any other activity is just not as valuable or as important as this job, based on your own priorities.

The more you discipline yourself to working nonstop on a single task, the more you progress along the "efficiency curve." You get more and more high-quality work done in less and less time.

Each time you stop working, however, you break this cycle and move back along the curve to where every part of the task is more difficult and time consuming.

Self-Discipline Is the Key

Elbert Hubbard defined self-discipline as "the ability to make yourself do what you should do, when you should do it, whether you feel like it or not."

In the final analysis, success in any area requires tons of discipline. Self-discipline, self-mastery, and self-control are the basic building blocks of character and high performance.

Starting a high-priority task and persisting with that task until it is 100 percent complete is the true test of your character, your willpower, and your resolve. Persistence is actually self-discipline in action. The good news is that the more you discipline yourself to persist on a major task, the more you like and respect yourself, and the higher is your self-esteem. And the more you like and respect yourself, the easier it is for you to discipline yourself to persist even more.

By focusing clearly on your most valuable task and concentrating single-mindedly until it is 100 percent complete, you actually shape and mold your own character. You become a superior person.

You feel stronger, more competent, more confident, and happier. You feel more powerful and productive.

You eventually feel capable of setting and achieving any goal. You become the master of your own destiny.

You place yourself on an ascending spiral of personal effectiveness on which your future is absolutely guaranteed.

And the key to all of this is for you to determine the most valuable and important thing you could possibly do at every single moment and then *Eat That Frog!*

EAT THAT FROG!

1. Take action! Resolve today to select the most important task or project that you could complete and then launch into it immediately.

2. Once you start your most important task, discipline yourself to persevere without diversion or distraction until it is 100 percent complete. See it as a test to determine whether you are the kind of person who can make a decision to complete something and then carry it out. Once you begin, refuse to stop until the job is finished.

Conclusion: Putting It All Together

The key to happiness, satisfaction, great success, and a wonderful feeling of personal power and effectiveness is for you to develop the habit of eating your frog first thing every day when you start work.

Fortunately, this is a learnable skill that you can acquire through repetition. And when you develop the habit of starting on your most important task before anything else, your success is assured.

Here is a summary of the twenty-one great ways to stop procrastinating and get more things done faster. Review these rules and principles regularly until they become firmly ingrained in your thinking and actions, and your future will be guaranteed.

1. **Set the table:** Decide exactly what you want. Clarity is essential. Write out your goals and objectives before you begin.

2. **Plan every day in advance:** Think on paper. Every minute you spend in planning can save you five or ten minutes in execution.

3. **Apply the 80/20 Rule to everything:** Twenty percent of your activities will account for 80 percent of your results. Always concentrate your efforts on that top 20 percent.

4. **Consider the consequences:** Your most important tasks and priorities are those that can have the most serious consequences, positive or negative, on your life or work. Focus on these above all else.

5. **Practice creative procrastination:** Since you can't do everything, you must learn to deliberately put off those tasks that are of low value so that you have enough time to do the few things that really count.

6. **Use the ABCDE Method continually:** Before you begin work on a list of tasks, take a few moments to organize them by value and priority so you can be sure of working on your most important activities.

7. **Focus on key result areas:** Identify and determine those results that you absolutely, positively have to get to do your job well, and work on them all day long.

8. **The Law of Three:** Identify the three things you do in your work that account for 90 percent of your contribution, and focus on getting them done before anything else. You will then have more time for your family and personal life.

9. **Prepare thoroughly before you begin:** Have everything you need at hand before you start. Assemble all the papers, information, tools, work materials, and numbers you might require so that you can get started and keep going.

10. **Take it one oil barrel at a time:** You can accomplish the biggest and most complicated job if you just complete it one step at a time.

11. **Upgrade your key skills:** The more knowledgeable and skilled you become at your key tasks, the faster you start them and the sooner you get them done.

12. **Leverage your special talents:** Determine exactly what it is that you are very good at doing, or could be very good at, and throw your whole heart into doing those specific things very, very well.

13. **Identify your key constraints:** Determine the bottlenecks or choke points, internal or external, that set the speed at which you achieve your most important goals, and focus on alleviating them.

14. **Put the pressure on yourself:** Imagine that you have to leave town for a month, and work as if you had to get all your major tasks completed before you left.

15. **Maximize your personal power:** Identify your periods of highest mental and physical energy each day, and structure your most important and demanding tasks around these times. Get lots of rest so you can perform at your best.

16. **Motivate yourself into action:** Be your own cheerleader. Look for the good in every situation. Focus

on the solution rather than the problem. Always be optimistic and constructive.

17. **Get out of the technological time sinks:** Use technology to improve the quality of your communications, but do not allow yourself to become a slave to it. Learn to occasionally turn things off and leave them off.

18. **Slice and dice the task:** Break large, complex tasks down into bite-sized pieces, and then do just one small part of the task to get started.

19. **Create large chunks of time:** Organize your days around large blocks of time where you can concentrate for extended periods on your most important tasks.

20. **Develop a sense of urgency:** Make a habit of moving fast on your key tasks. Become known as a person who does things quickly and well.

21. **Single handle every task:** Set clear priorities, start immediately on your most important task, and then work without stopping until the job is 100 percent complete. This is the real key to high performance and maximum personal productivity.

Make a decision to practice these principles every day until they become second nature to you. With these habits of personal management as a permanent part of your personality, your future success will be unlimited. Just do it! *Eat that frog!*

Index

Brian Tracy

SPEAKER, TRAINER, SEMINAR LEADER

Brian Tracy is one of the top professional speakers in the world, addressing more than 250,000 people each year throughout the United States, Europe, Asia, and Australia. Brian's keynote speeches, talks, and seminars are described as "inspiring, entertaining, informative, and motivational." His audiences include Fortune 500 companies and every size of business and association.

Call today for full information on booking Brian to speak at your next meeting or conference.

21st Century Thinking—How to outthink, outplan, and outstrategize your competition and get superior results in a turbulent, fast-changing business environment.

Advanced Selling Strategies—How to outthink, outperform, and outsell your competition using the most advanced strategies and tactics known to modern selling.

The Psychology of Success—How the top people think and act in every area of personal and business life. Countless practical, proven methods and strategies for peak performance.

Leadership in the New Millennium—How to apply the most powerful leadership principles ever discovered to manage, motivate, and get better results, faster than ever before.

Brian will carefully customize his talk for you and for your needs. Visit Brian Tracy International at www.brian tracy.com for more information, or call 858/481-2977 today for a free promotional package.

Brian Tracy's Personal Coaching Programs— The Keys to Making a Quantum Leap in Your Life and Career

Focal Point Advanced Coaching and Mentoring Program

Brian Tracy offers a personal coaching program in San Diego for successful entrepreneurs, self-employed professionals, and top salespeople. Participants learn how to apply the Focal Point Process to every part of their work and personal lives.

Participants learn a step-by-step process of personal strategic planning that enables them to take complete control of their time and their lives. Over the course of the program, participants meet with Brian Tracy one full day every three months. During these sessions, they learn how to double their income and double their time off.

They identify the things they enjoy doing the most and learn how to become better in their most profitable activities. Participants learn how to delegate, downsize, outsource, and eliminate all the tasks they neither enjoy nor benefit from. They learn how to identify their special talents and how to use leverage and concentration to move to the top of their fields.

Focal Point Personal Telephone Coaching Program

Brian Tracy's personally trained professional coaches work with you step-by-step to help you move to the next level of performance in your career.

This intensive twelve-week program comes complete with exercises, audio programs, prework, and personalized coaching.

You learn how to implement the Focal Point Process in every area of your life. Working with a trusted mentor, you develop complete clarity about who you are, what you want, where you are going, and the fastest ways to achieve all your goals.

For more information on the live or telephone coaching and mentoring programs offered by Brian Tracy, visit www.briantracy.com, call 858/481-2977, or write to Brian Tracy International, 462 Stevens Avenue, Suite 202, Solana Beach, CA 92075.

Visit Brian Tracy at www.21successsecrets.com for a free copy of his best-selling audio program, "The 21 Success Secrets of Self-Made Millionaires." You pay only shipping and handling.

Also, check out Brian Tracy's popular books *The 100 Absolutely Unbreakable Laws of Business Success* and *Goals!* at your local bookstore or at www.briantracy.com.

Brian Tracy University of
Sales and Entrepreneurship

Now you can learn the key skills you need to boost your sales and profitability.

Based on many years of experience with more than 1,000 businesses in forty-five countries, these powerful, practical courses in business, management, sales, and personal success teach you how to start, build, manage, or turn around any business.

You can learn the most important tools and techniques for achieving personal, sales, and business success at your computer—anytime, anywhere.

Each course consists of lessons presented classroom-style by Brian Tracy and includes reading materials, exercises, audio reinforcement, and the most advanced technology for accelerated learning.

COURSES INCLUDE

Increase Your Profits! (30 lessons)

Start Your Own Business (30 lessons)

Successful Selling (30 lessons)

High-Performance Leadership (30 lessons)

Maximum Performance (30 lessons)

Superior Sales Management (30 lessons)

Time Management for Results (12 lessons)

For complete information and free business or sales assessments, visit www.briantracy.com. Invest in your future today!

About the Author

Brian Tracy is a professional speaker, trainer, and consultant and is the chairman of Brian Tracy International, a training and consulting company based in Solana Beach, California. He is also a self-made millionaire.

Brian learned his lessons the hard way. He left high school without graduating and worked as a laborer for several years. He washed dishes, stacked lumber, dug wells, worked in factories, and stacked hay bales on farms and ranches.

In his mid-twenties, he became a salesman and began climbing up through the business world. Year by year, studying and applying every idea, method, and technique he could find, he worked his way up to become chief operating officer of a $265-million development company.

In his thirties, he enrolled at the University of Alberta and earned a bachelor of commerce degree; then he earned a masters in business administration from Andrew Jackson University. Over the years, he has worked in twenty-two different companies and industries. In 1981, he began teaching his success principles in talks and seminars around the country. Today, his books, audio programs, and video seminars have been translated into thirty-five languages and are used in fifty-two countries.

Brian has shared his ideas with more than 4 million people in forty-five countries since he began speaking professionally. He has served as a consultant and trainer for more than 1,000 corporations. He has lived and practiced every principle in this book. He has taken himself and countless thousands of other people from frustration and underachievement to prosperity and success.

Brian Tracy calls himself an "eclectic reader." He considers himself not an academic researcher but a synthesizer of information. Each year he spends hundreds of hours reading a wide variety of newspapers, magazines, books, and other materials. In addition, he listens to many hours of audio programs, attends countless seminars, and watches numerous videotapes on subjects of interest to him. Information gleaned from radio, television, and other media also adds to his knowledge base.

Brian assimilates ideas and information based on his own experience and that of others and incorporates them into his own experience. He is the bestselling author of more than forty books, including *Maximum Achievement, Advanced Selling Strategies, Focal Point,* and *The 100 Absolutely Unbreakable Laws of Business Success.* He has written and produced more than 300 audio and video learning programs that are used worldwide.

Brian is happily married and has four children. He lives on a golf course in San Diego. He travels and speaks more than 100 times each year and has business operations in seventeen countries. He is considered to be one of the foremost authorities on success and achievement in the world.

About Berrett-Koehler Publishers

Berrett-Koehler is an independent publisher dedicated to an ambitious mission: Creating a World That Works for All.

We believe that to truly create a better world, action is needed at all levels—individual, organizational, and societal. At the individual level, our publications help people align their lives with their values and with their aspirations for a better world. At the organizational level, our publications promote progressive leadership and management practices, socially responsible approaches to business, and humane and effective organizations. At the societal level, our publications advance social and economic justice, shared prosperity, sustainability, and new solutions to national and global issues.

A major theme of our publications is "Opening Up New Space." They challenge conventional thinking, introduce new ideas, and foster positive change. Their common quest is changing the underlying beliefs, mindsets, and structures that keep generating the same cycles of problems, no matter who our leaders are or what improvement programs we adopt.

We strive to practice what we preach—to operate our publishing company in line with the ideas in our books. At the core of our approach is stewardship, which we define as a deep sense of responsibility to administer the company for the benefit of all of our "stakeholder" groups: authors, customers, employees, investors, service providers, and the communities and environment around us.

We are grateful to the thousands of readers, authors, and other friends of the company who consider themselves to be part of the "BK Community." We hope that you, too, will join us in our mission.

A BK LIFE BOOK

This book is part of our BK Life series. BK Life books change people's lives. They help individuals improve their lives in ways that are beneficial for the families, organizations, communities, nations, and world in which they live and work. To find out more, visit www.bk-life.com.

Be Connected

Visit Our Website
Go to www.bkconnection.com to read exclusive previews and excerpts of new books, find detailed information on all Berrett-Koehler titles and authors, browse subject-area libraries of books, and get special discounts.

Subscribe to Our
Free E-Newsletter
Be the first to hear about new publications, special discount offers, exclusive articles, news about bestsellers, and more! Get on the list for our free e-newsletter by going to www.bkconnection.com.

Participate in the Discussion
To see what others are saying about our books and post your own thoughts, check out our blogs at www.bkblogs.com.

Get Quantity Discounts
Berrett-Koehler books are available at quantity discounts for orders of ten or more copies. Please call us toll-free at (800) 929-2929 or email us at bkp.orders@aidcvt.com.

Host a Reading Group
For tips on how to form and carry on a book reading group in your workplace or community, see our website at www .bkconnection.com.

Join the BK Community
Thousands of readers of our books have become part of the "BK Community" by participating in events featuring our authors, reviewing draft manuscripts of forthcoming books, spreading the word about their favorite books, and supporting our publishing program in other ways. If you would like to join the BK Community, please contact us at bkcommunity@bkpub.com.